C000072386

THE FORMATION OF THE
PAULINE CORPUS OF LETTERS

THE FORMATION OF THE
PAULINE CORPUS OF LETTERS

by

C. LESLIE MITTON

WIPF & STOCK · Eugene, Oregon

Wipf and Stock Publishers
199 W 8th Ave, Suite 3
Eugene, OR 97401

The Formation of the Pauline Corpus of Letters
By Mitton, C. Leslie
Copyright©1955 Epworth Press
ISBN 13: 978-1-60608-416-8
Publication date 01/02/2009
Previously published by Epworth Press, 1955

CONTENTS

INTRODUCTION

W E ARE curiously ignorant of the process by which Paul's letters were collected into the Corpus which won its way into the New Testament. Certain assumptions about it have been widely accepted in this country, but a vigorous challenge to them has in recent years been thrown out by two scholars of the United States of America. Owing, however, to contemporary difficulties of currency exchange, their works are not easily accessible, and are little known here.

This essay does not pretend to solve the problem, but to set forth the two types of answer, the conventional one and the unconventional, with the arguments by which they have been supported. If the latter is the more fully treated, it is because it is less generally known, and also because the writer believes it contains more truth than is usually allowed by British readers.

Since the manuscript was completed, Dr G. Zuntz's book on *The Text of the Epistles* has been published. In it he makes passing reference to Goodspeed's theory about the formation of the Pauline Corpus of letters, and declines to be persuaded by it. His comments, however, constitute more a denial than a refutation of the arguments. Readers are advised to consult what he has written on pp. 14 and 276-9 of his book.

I wish to thank my colleague, Rev. A. W. Wainwright, M.A., for kindly reading the proofs, and making several valuable suggestions.

C. L. MITTON

Handsworth College

April 1955

BIBLIOGRAPHY

Bauer, W.	(*RK*)	Rechtglaübigkeit und Ketzerei in ältesten Christentum.
Beare, F. W.	(*IP*)	First Epistle of Peter.
Charles, R. H.	(*ICC*)	International Critical Commentary on Revelation.
Charteris, A. H.	(*C*)	Canonicity.
Goodspeed, E. J.	(*CP*)	Christianity Goes to Press.
	(*FN*)	Formation of the New Testament.
	(*INT*)	Introduction to the New Testament.
	(*ME*)	The Meaning of Ephesians.
	(*NC*)	New Chapters in New Testament Study.
Harnack, A.	(*BAP*)	Die Briefsammlung des Apostels Paulus.
	(*ONT*)	Origin of the New Testament.
Harrison, P. N.	(*PP*)	The Problem of the Pastoral Epistles.
	(*PTE*)	Polycarp's Two Epistles to the Philippians.
Howard, W. F.	(*FG*)	The Fourth Gospel in Recent Criticism and Interpretation.
Kenyon, F. G.	(*RD*)	Recent Developments in the Textual Criticism of the Greek Bible.
	(*TG*)	The Text of the Greek Bible.
Knox, J.	(*MNT*)	Marcion and the New Testament.
	(*PLP*)	Philemon among the Letters of Paul.
Knox, W. L.	(*PCG*)	St Pāul and the Church of the Gentiles.
Lake, K.	(*EEP*)	The Earlier Epistles of St Paul.
Mitton, C. L.	(*EE*)	The Epistle to the Ephesians: Its Authorship, Origin and Purpose.
Moffatt, J.	(*ILNT*)	Introduction to the Literature of the New Testament.
Oxford Committee	(*NTAP*)	The New Testament in the Apostolic Fathers.
Selwyn, E. G.	(*IP*)	The First Epistle of St Peter.
Streeter, B. H.	(*FGG*)	The Four Gospels
	(*PC*)	The Primitive Church.
Westcott, B. F.	(*CNT*)	The Canon of the New Testament.
Westcott and Hort	(*WH*)	The New Testament in the Original Greek.
Zahn, Th.	(*GNK*)	Geschichte des neutestamentlichen Kanons.

CHAPTER ONE

THE FORMATION OF THE PAULINE CORPUS

THE COLLECTED letters of the Apostle Paul occupy a
pre-eminent place among the writings in the New
Testament. They claim no less than one quarter of its
total number of pages. That is an exceedingly large proportion
to come from the hand of one man, but it does not unfairly
represent the enormous influence which these letters have
exercised in the history of the Christian Church. Almost
every revival of religion which has cleansed and revitalized
the life of the Church has found a large part of its inspiration
and its vocabulary in these urgent and unpolished utterances
of this great Christian missionary.

Because of their supreme value, constant study has been
devoted to these letters, and the ceaseless investigations of
scholars have enabled us to provide reasonably probable
answers to most of the questions we ask about each individual
letter: Why it was written, when, where, and to whom? It is
true that even here some problems remain unsolved, but for
very many a convincing solution has been provided.

When, however, we turn from the letters as separate entities,
and begin to consider them as a collection, we find ourselves
beset with many still unanswered questions. We ask: Why
were the letters gathered together into the Corpus, as we
know it? *When* was it done? *Where* was it carried out? By
what process did the collection of letters reach its final form?
To whom should we give the credit for this enterprise of such
inestimable worth?

To no single one of these questions can an agreed answer be
given. It is true that possible answers have been suggested,
but they are speculative and unproved, based on a somewhat
subjective assessment of possibilities rather than on actual and
reliable evidence.

Indeed, the available evidence on which to base an answer

has sometimes seemed so slight that the most competent scholars have often declined to venture even a tentative answer. For instance, to our inquiry, '*When* was the Pauline Corpus formed?' Moffatt refuses to commit himself beyond this cautious reply: 'Whether this "Corpus Paulinum" can be dated as early as the age of Ignatius, or even earlier (as Zahn argues), is a question which can only be asked, in the paucity of the evidence available' (*ILNT*, p. 60). If we ask, '*Where* did it take place?', so great a scholar as Harnack is equally noncommittal. In his book on *The Origin of the New Testament* (p. 53) he writes: 'Much intensive study has been devoted to the problem presented by the compilation of the thirteen Pauline epistles with but meagre results. It is no longer possible to discover where the great final collection took place. From *1 Clement* we may be sure that a collection of several epistles then existed at Rome, and was treated so to speak as the public property of the Church. Twenty to thirty years later the collection was certainly in existence in several churches far distant from one another. This is enough for our purpose.'

If we ask further, '*How* did the individual letters come to be grouped together into a Corpus?', we find that a certain assumption has tended to find general acceptance, even though precise evidence in support of it is noticeably scarce. It is the assumption that the process by which the Corpus reached its final form was one of gradual, uninterrupted development. It is argued that the individual letters were recognized, immediately they were read, as documents of supreme value for the Church. They were not only treasured by their recipients, but given a place of permanent honour in the life of their community. They were read and re-read, again and again, and before long were accepted as appropriate material to be introduced into their services of corporate worship.

This gradual process is envisaged as taking place in one of two alternative ways. One group of scholars argues that, as individual churches who had received a Pauline letter learned of other churches who also possessed such a letter, an exchange of copies was arranged. In this way, a local collection of letters was from time to time increased by a new acquisition, until there came into existence in many different churches smaller or larger collections of the letters, varying from one another in the completeness of their contents, and continually being supplemented by letters acquired from other churches. At last, somewhere, one collection was complete, in that it contained all the letters addressed to churches, and in time all other collections were also brought up to the full complement.

A variant theory, though also based on the assumption that the process was one of gradual development, claims also that the individual letters were immediately valued by their recipients, and reverenced and even used publicly in the churches to which they had been sent. In time it came to be known that several such letters were possessed by individual churches. Perhaps, however, at first it was felt that their special value was restricted to the communities to whom they had been addressed. Only at a later stage did the idea gain ground that they might contain material of value for all the churches. As a result, a movement was set on foot to gather them all together, and make them available to the whole Church in a single Corpus.

This type of theory, asserting in one form or the other that the Corpus was the culminating stage in a gradual process of development, held the field almost unchallenged until recent years. It has now, however, been vigorously criticized in the writings of E. J. Goodspeed and John Knox. They assert that such evidence as is available points to something very different. Paul's letters, they argue, so far from gaining immediate and lasting popularity and authority in the early Church, actually fell into almost complete neglect, once they had served the original purpose for which they had first been written. Only a very few, out of the total number he must have written, survived at all, and these more by happy chance than by the deliberate intention of the churches which received them. Those which were not either destroyed or lost, were forgotten and left, idle and unremembered, either in some church safe or some church officer's cupboard. Indeed, as the years passed after Paul's death, his very name was in some danger of becoming for younger Christians only a vaguely familiar echo from the past.

This continued till about A.D. 90. About that time, an intimate disciple of the Apostle, who remembered his master with deep affection and enduring gratitude, and who, for personal reasons, knew of one or two of his surviving letters, was inspired to set on foot an inquiry to discover if any others were still in existence. His search met with remarkable success. Goodspeed draws a vivid and moving word-picture of this man, who has been able to discover several forgotten letters of the Apostle, and who is the first man ever to have the privilege of seeing and reading the collected Corpus, so familiar to us (*ME*, pp. 9ff)—'They overwhelm him with the force of a revelation'.

Goodspeed associates this theory of the origin of the first collection of Paul's letters with his own interpretation of the origin of the Epistle to the Ephesians, which he believes was compiled by this first collector to serve as a summary of Paul's main teaching, and was built up mainly from the contents of the other letters, with the purpose that it should stand first in the published Corpus, and serve as a kind of Introduction.

There is much to be said for this association of the origin of Ephesians with the publication of the collected letters of Paul, but our concern here is with the collected letters, and not with any individual item among them. Our purpose now, after this preliminary review of previously argued opinions, is to consider the arguments which have been used to support the theory of the gradual process, and to compare them with the newer arguments which urge that the Pauline Corpus came into existence as an act of deliberate purpose, an act which rescued the individual letters from obscurity, if not complete oblivion, and gave them back to the Church some thirty years or so after they had first been written.

The arguments of Goodspeed and Knox are well known in the United States of America, and widely accepted, but they are comparatively little known in Great Britain, and even where known have not always been treated with the seriousness they deserve.

It is not so much the aim of this book to reach a conclusion, as to present the evidence on which a conclusion may be based, and in particular to present the evidence which favours the newer interpretation.

We will review the older theories, taking as representatives of the two variants of it, on the one hand Kirsopp Lake and P. N. Harrison, and on the other hand Harnack. Before we notice the aspects in which they differ, we must consider that factor which they have in common, and in which they are both at variance with Goodspeed and Knox. This is the claim that Paul's letters were valued from the moment of their first reception, and treasured and used with increasing reverence in the community to which they were in the first place sent.

Harnack in 1926 published his *Die Briefsammlung des Apostels Paulus*, and gave us what, in spite of its brevity, was probably our best discussion, up to that time, of the formation of the Pauline Corpus. There he sought to present arguments to establish his opinion that Paul's letters were valued right from the moment of their first reception, and continued to receive from their recipients continuous, and even increasing, reverence. He makes these four main points:

(*a*) So great was the epistolary skill of Paul, that each recipient of a letter must have realized immediately that it was of immense value, and something to be greatly treasured.

(*b*) We know that the power of his letters was realized at once, because of what his opponents said of them: 'His letters are weighty and strong; but his bodily presence is weak, and his speech is of no account' (2 Co 10¹⁰). They also rebuke him for misusing his skill as a letter-writer (2 Co 10⁹, 3¹).

(*c*) The churches brought into being by Paul's preaching and organizing power were linked together by their attachment to him and governed by the same principles. This is apparent from 1 Co 7¹⁷: 'And so ordain I in all the churches.' This implies that the apostle wrote frequent communications for their guidance.

(*d*) So influential were Paul's letters, that enemies, seeking to undermine his work, appear to have issued false ones in his name (cf. 2 Th 2², 3¹⁷). (*BAP*, pp. 7-8.)

These arguments show that Paul's letters made a great impression on those who first received them, but do they prove more than that? It cannot be said that they show beyond question that this impression also in fact at once led the local church to accord to the letter a permanent and honoured place in the life of the community. Even documents which make an initial impact on contemporaries can easily be forgotten and neglected after the passage of some years.

Indeed, if Harnack's third point is true, and Paul's correspondence was indeed very large (as is most probable), much larger in fact than the small number of letters still surviving, it implies that many letters have been completely lost. Harnack indeed seeks to meet this point by suggesting that the smallness of the number is due to an act of deliberate selection from a much greater number. This, however, does not appear probable. It is much less likely that, at the end of the first century, ten of Paul's surviving letters should have been chosen from the others, and the rest irretrievably destroyed, than that at a much earlier date they should have been forgotten and lost. And if so many were neglected and lost, is it not possible that the few that survived were neglected, but by some happy chance not completely lost?

Kirsopp Lake, starting from the same assumption as Harnack, that the letters from the first became a treasured possession of the churches which received them, outlines his theory of the formation of the Pauline Corpus. He believes that first of all small and partial collections came into existence in various centres, before the Corpus in its completed form finally replaced them. He conjectures that one church, which had received a letter from Paul, heard of a similar letter in some neighbouring church, and exchanged a copy of its own for a copy of its neighbours'. As a result of this process, several churches came to have small collections of their own, by no means identical with each other. Lake finds evidence for this not only in the Apostolic Fathers, but also in the diversity of some of the lists in later writers (*EEP*, pp. 356-8). The list of Marcion, the Muratorian Canon, Tertullian and Origen do not, for instance, exactly coincide. He quotes this as evidence that their collections of the letters had grown up independently in different centres, and in consequence did not contain precisely the same letters, and certainly did not arrange them in the same order.

No one can contradict the facts which Lake records. The earliest lists arrange the letters with considerable diversity of order. The significance of the order in some of the lists will be the subject of our consideration at a later stage, and an attempt will be made to ascertain what the original order was, if indeed it is permissible to speak of one original order, and not, as Lake argues, of several equally original but varying orders.

The contents of the lists also vary. Marcion's list did not include the Pastoral Epistles; the Muratorian Canon did. The epistles actually named by Tertullian and Origen are fewer than those in the complete list of the Muratorian Canon. It is, however, not permissible to argue that because these two Christian leaders do not mention or use this or that letter, therefore they had no knowledge of it. It is quite possible to be well acquainted with a document, and nevertheless have no occasion to mention it or quote from it. Tertullian and Origen may well have had the complete collection and merely by chance may have happened to mention some and not all of them. Lake, however, feels justified in interpreting these omissions as evidence of the existence of various independent collections in different centres. He writes: 'We find that this variety of order in the list of the Epistles is accompanied by variations in the text, and the most natural conclusion is that we have to deal with various collections of the Pauline Epistles . . . so that we have to recognize that there never was any "original" text but that various churches had their own collections, each with its own text' (*EEP*, p. 358).

Streeter also, in his earlier book, *The Four Gospels*, gives his support to the theory that the Pauline Corpus reached its final form by stages. He writes: 'We can trace four stages in the growth of the Roman "*Corpus Paulinum*"—the nucleus (Rom., 1 Cor., Eph., perhaps Phil.) known already to Clement, A.D. 96; the Ten (Marcion's Canon), *c.* 140; the Thirteen (adding 1 and 2 Tim., Tit.) before 200 (Muratorian Canon); the Fourteen, including Hebrews, *c.* A.D. 350' (*FGG*, pp. 526-7). It need not be questioned that the Pastorals were included later than the other ten, and Hebrews still later; but the fact that Clement's epistle shows traces of only

B

four of the ten cannot be accepted as conclusive evidence that these four are the only ones that Clement knew. There is no ground for supposing that he did not know all ten, merely because he omitted to quote from them all in his epistle. In his later book (*The Primitive Church*), however, Streeter makes most sympathetic and favourable reference to Goodspeed's theory of the formation of the Pauline Corpus, and his suggestion that its collection was prompted by the appearance of the Acts of the Apostles (*PC*, pp. 159ff). His earlier opinion, therefore, as expressed in the *Four Gospels*, may not represent his final judgement.

P. N. Harrison, also (in *PTE*, pp. 235-9), gives careful consideration to the method by which the Pauline Corpus was formed, and agrees substantially with Lake. He concludes that it came into being by stages, several smaller collections preceding and leading up to the first complete one. He asks: 'Why should it not have happened like other great things, step by step?' (p. 238). But to argue that it might have happened so, is not the same as proving that it did. To our question, therefore, how our collection of Pauline epistles took shape, he gives this reply: 'Not, it would seem, by any single operation carried out within any short interval of time, but as the result of a gradual process over a period of years. So much at least is strongly suggested both by the evidence and the inherent probability, in the absence of any explicit contemporary record' (p. 235). In the reconstruction of the proposed stages, Harrison seems to rely more on what he calls 'the inherent probability' than on actual evidence. This is a legitimate line of approach, provided that we never let it assume the authority of a conclusion based on proved evidence. Goodspeed, no doubt, would also argue for his contrary theory that it corresponds with 'inherent probability'.

Harrison's reconstruction of the actual process is as follows: The nucleus of a collection already existed in the several letters addressed to Corinth. To these were added in time the letter to the Romans. This would be natural enough in view of the close connexion between the two churches at the time when *1 Clement* was written. Then would come the acquisition of the epistles to the churches in Macedonia—'Philippians' and

'Thessalonians'. This would form a 'European Corpus'. The Corinthians would naturally turn next to the leaders at Ephesus, who would be able to introduce them to other letters known in Asia Minor—'Galatians', 'Colossians', Romans 16, and 'Philemon'. Harrison concludes his reconstruction with these words: 'With the materials so assembled before him, some Christian teacher in Ephesus may well have been prompted, as Goodspeed suggests, to write that wonderful exposition which we know as Ephesians, where the authentic thoughts of the Apostle are carried to their logical development, and shown in their application to any and every church within that larger body now conceived as a unity and as a whole' (*PTE*, pp. 239-40). This theory of a gradual process, therefore, in the formation of the Pauline Corpus, though differing from Goodspeed's, does not exclude his explanation of the origin and purpose of Ephesians.

Harnack, as we have seen, agrees with Lake and Harrison in thinking that Paul's letters made an instantaneous impression on their first readers, and from that moment held and increased their influence in that community. He differs from them, however, in emphatically denying that there is any evidence at all that incomplete and partial collections of the letters ever existed, or that individual letters had any separate circulation of their own.[1] He recognizes, however, that the original collection, as known to Marcion, contained only ten letters, and that the three Pastorals were added later. He believes that this collection was in existence before the end of the first century, and, after discussing the possibility that it may have existed earlier, gives it as his opinion that it should be allocated to the last quarter of the century.[2] The main reason for this conclusion is the complete absence from Acts of any sign of acquaintance with Paul's letters. Interestingly enough, it is this very fact which Goodspeed makes one of the chief supports for his own, rather different theory.

---

[1] '*Fest steht, dass kein einziger echter Paulusbrief seine selbständige Überlieferung hat und dass wir auch von kleineren Teilsammlungen nichts wissen; vielmehr sind uns die Briefe sämtlich, wie die Handschriften beweisen, als gesammelte überliefert*' (Harnack, *BAP*, p. 6).

[2] '*Man wird also das letzte Viertel des I. Jahrhunderts für die Entstehung der Sammlung der 10 und, gegen Ende dieses Zeitraums, auch der 13 Briefe offen lassen müssen*' (Harnack, *BAP*, p. 7).

It might be expected that the writings of the Apostolic Fathers would throw some light on our problem, since apart from the New Testament books themselves, they are our earliest Christian writings, though, even here, we could not expect much, for the earliest of the Fathers wrote at a time later than the date when Paul's letters had been collected, if not in the final form of thirteen letters, at any rate in that of the ten.

In fact, the evidence they provide is completely indecisive. In many cases it cannot be determined with complete certainty whether a particular Father reveals acquaintance with a particular Pauline letter or not. The verdict often has to be based not on unmistakable fact, but on a somewhat subjective interpretation of rather elusive evidence, with the result that scholars are not agreed on its significance. Moreover, even if we can be quite definite that no trace of a particular Pauline letter can be found in one particular Father, this proves merely that he fails to quote from it or refer to it; it does not necessarily mean that he did not know it. As Goodspeed puts it: 'Few people who possess all Paul's letters make use of them all in a single letter or group of letters. It is wrong' [because they fail to quote them] 'to infer that the Apostolic Fathers did not possess all Paul's letters, but used a collection of Paul's letters from which some were absent'.

It will, however, be wise for us to have before us such evidence as can be drawn from the writings of these Fathers of the Church. Nowhere is it more impartially presented than in *The New Testament in the Apostolic Fathers*, a record of the combined research of a Committee of distinguished Oxford scholars. There is clearly indicated the extent of the probability that Paul's various letters are quoted or echoed in these sub-apostolic writings.

This Committee first enumerates the similarities which are capable of being interpreted as evidence of some kind of literary dependence, and then seeks to grade them. If they are such as to furnish conclusive proof that a particular Pauline letter has been known and used, they are classed as 'A'. If the proof they furnish is less than conclusive, but highly probable, their class mark is 'B'. Rather less than probable, but nevertheless quite likely echoes of Paul are marked as 'C', whereas

'D' means that the similarity can be regarded as indicating only a possible, not probable acquaintance. From the gradings of the various individual similarities with any one Pauline epistle, a further grading can be given for each epistle as a whole.

In individual cases careful study may lead to a modification of the Committee's judgement, but their verdict is the considered opinion of six highly competent scholars working in close co-operation, and availing themselves of the investigations of earlier scholars. Since it represents several minds and not just one, and since it is also an independent work, and not related to the proving of some particular theory, it is free from the dangers of individual prejudice. Their combined judgement is marked at all times by a deliberate caution. No probability is overstated. Rather it is understated.

The following table summarizes their opinions:

	A	B	C	D
Barnabas (? Alexandria)	—	Rom.	Eph.	1 Cor. 2 Cor. Col. Tit. 1 Tim. 2 Tim.
Didache (?? Syria)	—	—	—	? Rom. ? 1 Cor.
1 Clement (Rome)	Rom. 1 Cor.	—	Tit.	2 Cor. Gal. Philp. Col. 1 Tim.
Ignatius (Antioch and Asia Minor)	1 Cor.	Eph.	Rom. 2 Cor. Gal. Philp. 1 and 2 Tim. Tit.	Col. Philm. (?) 1 and 2 Thess. (?)
Polycarp (Asia Minor)	1 Cor.	Rom. 2 Cor. Gal. Eph. Philp. 2 Thess. 1 and 2 Tim.	—	Col.
Hermas (Rome)	—	1 Cor. Eph.	—	Rom. 1 Thess.
2 Clement	—	—	—	1 Cor. Eph.

The provenance of several of these sub-apostolic writings is a matter of dispute, and only tentative conclusions may be based on any opinion about it.

Since this book was published, other scholars have made

specialized studies which are relevant to our inquiry, and reference must be made to one or two of them.

P. N. Harrison has made a most careful study of Ignatius and Polycarp, and he regards it as quite certain that both of them were familiar with Ephesians. He is, however, unconvinced that Ignatius refers to any Pauline letter other than 1 Corinthians and Ephesians. He seeks to find an explanation for this strange fact that it is these two letters only which are reflected in the letters of Ignatius. He suggests that 1 Corinthians had a private circulation before the publication of the Pauline Corpus, and so had been known to Ignatius separately for some time; and that Ephesians had come to his notice in the recently published Pauline Corpus, and alone among all the letters had attracted his special notice and won his immediate approval because of its emphasis on Christian unity (*PTE*, p. 246). Harrison also dissents from the Oxford Committee's assessment of the relationship between Ignatius and the Pastoral Epistles. He allows that certain genuine Pauline fragments, later incorporated in the Pastorals, may have been included in the original Corpus and thus have been known to Ignatius. The great majority of the correspondences, however, he believes to be due to the acquaintance of the compiler of the Pastorals with the letters of Ignatius. The Pastorals in their present form, he believes, were subsequent to the letters of Ignatius. Moreover, J. Knox in *Philemon among the Letters of Paul*, has made out a very strong case for his opinion that Ignatius definitely knew Paul's letter to Philemon, and used it in writing to the church at Ephesus.

With these modifications we avail ourselves of the Oxford Committee's findings. It is clear that 1 Corinthians is the letter of Paul which has most clearly impressed itself on the minds of the early Christian leaders. This epistle is confidently known early in the second century in the churches of Rome and Asia Minor, and perhaps in Syria. Ephesians is rather less familiar, but still known, in Rome, Asia Minor and Alexandria. Romans is known at Rome and Alexandria, but becomes prominent in Asia Minor only by the time of Polycarp. We have already been reminded that the absence of specific reference cannot be interpreted as lack of acquaintance, but it is justifiable to insist that those epistles which are quoted most frequently are those which have most vividly impressed their readers. The prominence of 1 Corinthians and Ephesians, which even take precedence over Romans, is unexpected and noteworthy, and deserves special inquiry. The explanation which Harrison gave for their predominance in Ignatius's letters will not hold good for Barnabas and Hermas as well. Another explanation, with an equal claim to consideration, will be suggested later.

If failure to quote from a Pauline letter proved ignorance of it, the evidence of the Apostolic Fathers would support Lake and Harrison in the claim that partial collections existed in different centres, before the complete Corpus was formed. It does not however prove this. Any one of the Apostolic Fathers may have known all ten epistles without happening to reflect more than one or two.

In spite of minor divergences, however, the general assumption, as we have seen, has been that the Pauline Corpus was formed as a last stage in a long and gradual process, by which the individual letters had become increasingly familiar and influential. It is against this background that Goodspeed's theory has been propounded. An outline of his conclusions and the arguments on which they are based is given in Chapter 13 of his *Introduction to the New Testament* under the title: 'The First Collection of Paul's Letters.' J. Knox also, in Chapter 3 of his book on *Marcion and the New Testament*, under the heading of 'The Pauline Corpus', provides an illuminating study of the subject, and corroborates and supplements the theory which Goodspeed has put forward. They both believe that the letters of Paul did not 'trickle' into circulation, but were brought to the notice of the Church at large by a deliberate act of publication. They claim that the letters were, for the most part, forgotten after they had been read by their first recipients, when the situation which caused them to be written had ceased to exist; so that the Church as a whole was completely unaware of them, and quite uninfluenced by them, till someone set himself to collect them, and then to publish them. The evidence for this they find not so much in the Apostolic Fathers as in the New Testament itself. Those books in the New Testament which can with some confidence be dated before A.D. 90 show not the slightest acquaintance with Paul's letters, though these had been written before A.D. 60, and, according to the current theory, had been immediately recognized as of great and permanent value, and very soon formed into local collections. The absence of explicit references to (or quotations from) the Pauline epistles in these early writings would not be so remarkable were it not that the books of the New Testament which were written after A.D. 90 show a clear knowledge of them, and not of one or two only, but of them all.

It is this sudden jump from total ignorance to knowledge of all ten that seems to require the explanation that for a considerable period Paul's letters were largely forgotten, and then, quite suddenly, they came to public notice by an act of publication.

Can this claim that for a generation Paul's letters were almost entirely neglected be maintained in face of the arguments that Harnack used to uphold the opposite conclusion?

Harnack certainly shows that Paul's letters exercised great influence on the situations to which they were primarily addressed. It is doubtful, however, whether his arguments can be taken as proving that they continued, without any interruption, to be reverenced as expressions of abiding truth. The fact that a letter makes a decisive contribution at a critical juncture of events does not mean that that letter will remain influential for many years to follow.

Further, there are points in Harnack's statement of the relevant facts to be borne in mind, which accord well with Goodspeed's interpretation of them. For instance, Harnack recognizes that in the Acts of the Apostles there is no trace of the use of any of the Pauline epistles.[3] This for him is decisive against the suggestion that Paul himself arranged for his letters to be collected. Indeed he assumes that it can only mean that the collection was not made until after the writing of Acts. For this reason he allocates the formation of the complete Corpus to the last quarter of the first century.

---

[3] '. . . weil in der Apostelgeschichte die Benutzung keines Paulusbriefes nachgewiesen werden kann' (BAP, p. 7).

We may ask, however, whether this complete silence on the part of Acts does not suggest that at that time the letters were not only not collected but that even individually they were largely unknown. Would Acts have been so completely silent, if they were as well known in certain important churches as Harnack suggests? Is it likely that the collection of the letters would have been delayed as late as A.D. 90 if the individual letters had for so long been known and influential in prominent centres, and even used there in public worship?

We have seen that Harnack differs from Lake and others in doubting the existence of partial collections in different localities. If, however, the letters were valued from the first, as Harnack suggests, is it not probable that they would soon have come to be associated in groups? If such groups did not in fact exist, does it not suggest that the letters were not generally known until they were for the first time brought out in a complete collection?

We saw, too, that Harnack was compelled to assume that the ten letters in the first collection were a deliberate selection from a much larger number that was available, though, if that is true his arguments for the inclusion of Philemon are not convincing. It is, however, difficult to resist the conclusion that these ten letters, when they were collected, were all the letters which were available. If this is so, does it not point to the probability that many other letters had been lost? And if many had been lost through indifference, is it not possible that those which survived had at any rate been long neglected or overlooked?

One feature at least of these extant letters points to this conclusion. It is that they are not in the form in which Paul first sent them. There are dislocations and insertions. It is not merely that two letters to the same address have been joined together to form one, which would be natural enough, but parts of one letter appear embedded in another. A letter is referred to in 1 Co 5⁹ which is no longer known to us as a separate letter, but many scholars are persuaded that part, if not all, of it has found its way into 2 Corinthians at 6¹⁴-7¹. Again at 2 Co 7⁸ an epistle is mentioned which does not correspond with any separate epistle known to us, but strong arguments have been brought forward to show that Chapters

10-12 in 2 Corinthians may well be identified with this very epistle. If this is so then 2 Corinthians has not come down to us in precisely the same form as it left the hand of Paul. Again, Romans 16 is widely thought to be a separate letter, probably addressed to Ephesus, which came to be added to the main body of Romans. Perhaps also part of Romans 15 should be regarded in the same way. In Philippians, the section 3^{1b}-4^3 reads like an intrusion. Not only does 3^{1b} lack any conceivable connexion with the preceding words, but it is very noticeable that 4^4 would follow on from 3^{1a} with complete naturalness. All these dislocations have been generally accepted as demonstrated. Vincent Taylor, in a footnote to his article in the *Hibbert Journal* (1950) on Loisy's *Origin of the New Testament*, is only summarizing the consensus of opinion among scholars when he allows that 2 Co 10-12, 2 Co 6^{14}-7^1, Ro 15^{14-33}, Ro 16^{1-23} (?) and Ph 3^{1b}-4^3 may be regarded as 'parts of earlier letters'. It is doubtful, however, if these are all the dislocations. A lost letter is referred to in Col 4^{16}, where Paul makes mention of a letter of his which will reach Colossæ 'from Laodicea'. It is true that Goodspeed wishes to identify it with the letter we call 'Philemon', and others argue that it is the letter known to us as 'Ephesians'. This second suggestion is most unlikely, and the first is little more than an interesting guess. A further dislocation is almost certainly to be found at 2 Co 2^{14}. In the preceding verses, in self-explanation, Paul is giving a careful account of his actions. He has told of the restless anxiety for Titus's return from Corinth which kept him from patiently awaiting his arrival at Troas, and then drove him on into Macedonia in hope of meeting Titus the sooner. Then the urgent narrative breaks off, to be resumed at 7^5 with a description of harassing trouble in Macedonia and at last the relief and joy of Titus's arrival and the good news he brought. In Paul's original letter, 7^5 would follow 2^{13}, and the intervening verses may be regarded as a further instance of an insertion from another Pauline letter.

These features of the letters suggest that they had not been individually treasured and preserved with the utmost care, but rather that they had been treated with a measure of indifference and neglect, with the result that the individual sheets had disintegrated, and it was left to a collector to rearrange them as best he could. His interest would be spiritual truth and not historical and literary accuracy, and so the errors in arrangement would be less noticeable to him than to us. If, however, the letters had been valued from the first as Harnack suggests, it is not likely that they would have suffered this degree of disarrangement.

In his earlier treatment of the Pauline Corpus in his *Origin of the New Testament*, Harnack claimed not only that the letters were valued from the time of their arrival, but even that they were given a place in public worship from earliest times. Starting from a statement of Dionysius, Bishop of Corinth about A.D. 170, that Clement's letter was still read, Harnack continues: 'If this happened in the case of important letters between the churches, what doubt can there be that it was so also, above all, with the epistles of Paul—so unique, so incomparable—in Corinth and Rome, in Philippi and Thessalonica, in Ephesus, Hierapolis and Colossæ, and not only in these places but wherever collections of Pauline epistles had arrived' (*ONT*, p. 27).[4] But what was customary in A.D. 170 or even earlier in A.D. 95 cannot be assumed to apply equally to A.D. 60. Goodspeed is emphatic in his denial of what Harnack assumes on the basis of 'inherent probability': 'The widespread idea that Paul's letters or the best of them sprang immediately into general influence and circulation, is at variance, not only with the probabilities, but with the facts' (*CP*, p. 15). It is on the complete absence of any echo of Paul's writings in Mark, Matthew and Luke-Acts that Goodspeed bases his reversal of earlier opinions. Particularly is the complete silence of Acts most strange, if Paul was already known as the writer of treasured letters. Even if some correspondences between Acts and Ephesians can be recognized, it can by no means be taken for granted that it was the author of Acts who knew the epistle. It is almost certainly the other way round.[5]

---

[4] So also in *BAP*, p. 11: '*Die Sammlung der Briefe kann schlechterdings nur denselben Zweck gehabt haben, der ursprünglich jedem einzelnen Brief für die Gemeinde zukam, an die er gerichtet war: sie sollte fort und fort in der Brüderschaft öffentlich gelesen werden, um sie in ihrem Christenstande zu belehren, zu leiten, zu festigen und zum Ausharren zu bewegen.*'

[5] See *Epistle to the Ephesians* by C. L. Mitton, chapter XVIII.

As for the other epistles, there is no sure ground for saying that any one of them is echoed in Acts. It is true that Streeter (*PC*, p. 160) hazards the opinion that Luke knew Romans (cf. also *FGG*, p. 555) and 1 Corinthians, and that these two epistles were widely circulated from a very early date. He does not, however, give evidence to bear out this personal impression, and on the main issue he does not disagree with Goodspeed, for he writes: 'It is hard to believe that Luke himself when he wrote Acts *c.* A.D. 85 had access to the complete collection of the epistles of Paul; and if Luke did not possess them all, who else would?' (*PC*, p. 160). So, too, Goodspeed argues: 'With all his interest in Paul and admiration for him, Luke has no acquaintance with his letters. . . . The Gospel Literature, Mark, Matthew and Luke-Acts, shows no influence of Paul's letters' (*INT*, pp. 210-11). He summarizes his position thus: 'The old traditional idea that the Pauline letters leaked into gradual circulation is inexorably negatived by the ignorance of the Synoptists of any such literature. . . . The united testimony of Matthew, Mark, Luke, puts the matter beyond peradventure; when they wrote, the letters of Paul had disappeared from Christian consciousness. Certainly some of them existed in old files, or church chests, but they were not present to the current life and thought of the church from A.D. 65 to 90. They were forgotten' (*NC*, p. 63).

This may seem a startling declaration. Paul occupies so prominent a place in our New Testament that it is difficult for us to imagine that anyone, having once read his letters, should fail to see the immense significance of them, not just for the immediate local situation but for the enduring needs of the Church as well. More than a quarter of our New Testament bears the name of Paul. No other single person plays so large a part. But that was a position that had to be won; it was not instantly the unanimous judgement of the churches. 'It is undeniable that Paul bulks larger in the New Testament than he bulked in the life of the early second century', writes J. Knox (*MNT*, p. 36). Nor was this lack of appreciation confined to the very early years of the second century. There is good reason to believe, not only that Paul's letters were ignored for a generation, but that even after their publication, they were in some parts held in considerable suspicion. Further on in the same book, Knox writes: 'Paul was at one time in danger of being lost to the heretics. Neither Justin nor Papias (so far as we know) so much as refers to Paul' (p. 115). 'This silence . . . can most naturally be interpreted to mean that in some churches at least Paul must have come under suspicion.' In fact, the greatest obstacle to the acceptance of Paul as a writer of full canonical authority appears to have been, not the early neglect of his epistles, nor yet the hesitation of those who interpreted the Christian Faith rather differently from him, but the hearty approval which some of the heretics gave to his writings. Marcion in particular found much in Paul to support his particular interpretation of Christ's message and significance, and claimed Paul as the prophet of his own innovations. This caused great embarrassment to the Church leaders, and seems to have forced them to make a decision. Paul must either be declared a heretic like Marcion, or he must be given the full approval of the Church's leaders, and be shown to have been misused by Marcion. The second was the alternative chosen, and it may very well be that this acceptance of Paul's writings as authoritative was the first clear act in the formation of what later came to be the canon of the New Testament.

So far, then, from Paul's letters being always the object of universal reverence in the Christian churches, it may well have been that they were at first overlooked, and then rescued from general neglect by a bold act of collection and publication. Even then, though exercising a powerful influence, they were not accorded universal approval. Marcion, however, forced the Church to abandon any attitude of hesitation and to follow the lead of the church of Asia Minor (represented by Polycarp) and give her full approval to the letters, though probably with additions that made the enlarged edition more acceptable to the temper of that day than the earlier and smaller collection, which had been championed by Marcion. In particular, the Pastoral Epistles were probably added, and possibly also some passages in the ten Epistles which seem to have been missing from the copies which Marcion used.

Our concern here is, however, not with the later embarrassment which the Church experienced as a result of Marcion's attempt to monopolize Paul, but with the long period of neglect into which his epistles appear to have lapsed between A.D. 60 and 90.

If indeed it is probable that they suffered general neglect for thirty years, can evidence be produced to show that after that time they came into public knowledge through some renewed interest in Paul, not one by one, but all together, the whole ten of them, including Ephesians, but excluding the Pastorals?

Evidence can be produced. It consists in the fact that by the turn of the century these letters were no longer unknown or ignored, but were quoted, and were influential enough to affect to a considerable degree the writings of other Christians about this time. Moreover all ten of the letters were known and influential, both individually and as a collected corpus.

Goodspeed and J. Knox agree in basing these conclusions on three grounds:

(1) The writings of the New Testament which were written after A.D. 90 all reflect a knowledge of this Pauline Corpus. Goodspeed, after describing the complete absence in the earlier writings of anything which suggests a knowledge of Paul's letters, continues: 'But from this point on the situation is reversed. Every Christian document shows acquaintance with Paul's letters—Revelation, Hebrews, *1 Clement*, 1 Peter, Ignatius, Polycarp, John. This is in fact the key to the later literature of the New Testament; it is all written in the presence of the collected Pauline letters. Over against the total non-acquaintance of the earlier evangelists the difference is positively glaring. Before the publication of Luke-Acts, nobody knew them; after the appearance of Luke-Acts, everybody knows them' (*INT*, p. 211). Elsewhere he adds: 'This familiarity continues to colour Christian writings steadily thereafter, through James, the Pastorals, 2 Peter—all the rest of the New Testament' (*CP*, p. 49).

(2) The unexpected convention of the letter-form, which is so generally adopted after A.D. 90, requires an explanation. Paul's letters are probably the only real letters in the New Testament, though so many other writings have the form of letters. In reality, however, these others are treatises or sermons arranged as if they were letters. The most probable

explanation of this curious convention is that the publication of Paul's letters had established a precedent which others felt, obliged to follow. Hebrews, *1 Clement*, 1 Peter, Ignatius, Polycarp, Barnabas, Jude, 2 Peter, John, the Pastorals, by producing what they have to say in the form of a letter, bear witness to the strength of this precedent and the convention it established. Even Revelation is prefaced by a series of letters which make a very odd introduction to an apocalypse. Even the dissertation of James, in order to be acceptable to the Christian public, had to be made into a letter. This 'shower of Christian letters', as Goodspeed calls them, is strong evidence that soon after the publication of Luke-Acts Paul's letters exercised a dominant influence in the Christian Church.

(3) The practice of publishing groups of letters in corpus-form requires the Pauline Corpus to explain it. For, shortly after A.D. 90, we find not only the convention of the letter form, but the custom of making collections of letters and of issuing them as collections. Revelation, for instance, opens with seven letters, one addressed to each of seven churches, preceded by an introductory letter to all seven. So far as we can tell, these individual letters had no separate existence. Their first appearance was in this collected form, with the general letter of introduction preceding. That is, they were written and published as a corpus from the very beginning. Not long afterwards we find Polycarp collecting the letters of Ignatius into a Corpus for distribution among the Christian communities. It almost seems as though this step had been part of the writer's intention from the first, for copies of the seven letters were conveniently available. Further, it is a curious fact, which surely is something more than a strange coincidence, that the number of the collected letters of Ignatius is seven, just as the letters which introduce 'Revelation' number seven.

Both J. Knox (*MNT*, p. 57) and Streeter (*PC*, pp. 159-60) agree with Goodspeed that it was the publication of the Pauline Corpus which 'led to the production and circulation of other corpuses of letters' (*INT*, p. 219). Streeter's opinion is that 'the existence of this demand for a collection of the letters of Ignatius is explicable only if the Pauline Corpus had familiarized that church (Philippi) with the idea of, and created the demand for, collected Letters by Christian saints' (*PC*, p. 161).

Of these three arguments, the first is likely to be the most convincing. Indeed it will be almost conclusive, if the claim it makes can be definitely established, that Revelation, Hebrews, 1 Peter, John, James, the Pastorals, 2 Peter, as well as *1 Clement*, Ignatius and Polycarp, all exhibit a knowledge of all the letters of the Pauline Corpus. Goodspeed conveniently tabulates the extent to which each of these writings displays familiarity with the Pauline epistles. This table is printed in his *Introduction to the New Testament*, p. 213, and 'owes much to the one prepared by Dr A. E. Barnett in his elaborate study, *The Use of the Letters of Paul in Pre-Catholic Christian Literature* (p. 612)'. Ephesians itself is also quoted as evidence of the corpus, since it reveals acquaintance with the other nine letters of Paul.

	Rev	Heb	Clem	1 Pet	Jn	Ign	Pol	Jas	Marc	Past	2 P.
Eph	x	x	x	x	x	x	x	.x	x	x	x
Rom	x	x	x	x	x	x	x	x	x	x	x
1 Cor	x	x	x		x	x	x	x	x	x	x
2 Cor	x		x	x	x	x		x	x	x	x
Gal	x	x	x	x	x	x	x	x	x	x	x
Phlp	x	x	x		x	x	x	x	x	x	x
Col	x	x	x		x	x			x	x	x
1 Th	x	x	x		x	x	x	x	x	x	x
2 Th	x			x	x		x		x	x	x
Phlm	x	x			x	x			x	x	x

In the above table, 'x' indicates what is claimed to be reliable evidence that the particular Pauline letter so marked was familiar to the writer under whose name it appears. The makers of this table certainly accept as positive proof evidence which the Oxford Committee, for instance, regarded as indecisive. This does not, however, necessarily mean that the table is unreliable, because we have seen some reason to regard the Oxford Committee's conclusions as erring on the side of caution. We should, however, on the other hand, be wise to regard this table as probably erring a little in the direction of over-confidence. Even then it is impressive, and may be taken, even by a cautious interpreter, as evidence of the appearance of the Pauline Corpus somewhere about A.D. 90.

It is possible that some may argue that even this evidence is not inconsistent with a theory of varying collections of the letters in different areas, each with a slightly different content. The further evidence from (3) on page 31 is however strongly corroborative of the one corpus of ten letters. That the letter corpus in Revelation and the letter corpus of Ignatius (with an introductory letter from Polycarp) should both follow the same pattern of seven letters addressed to individual destinations and an eighth of a general introductory type, strongly suggests that they are both moulded to a pattern, and that the pattern is the Pauline Corpus. What evidence is there that this Corpus had some such constitution as this?

There is good reason to believe that in the first collection of Paul's letters, the two letters to Corinth were not separated, but grouped together in one unit. So too were the letters to Thessalonica. Marcion seems to have known them in that way. What we know, therefore, as the ten would appear as eight. If, therefore, as Goodspeed claims, Ephesians was an introductory epistle, preparing the way for the other seven, the pattern which Ignatius and the author of Revelation followed is clear. Even if this position for Ephesians is not conceded, that does not necessarily invalidate the argument, for it may have been that Colossians and Philemon were also treated as a single unit. There is some evidence pointing in this direction. In that case, what we know as the ten letters would appear as seven, with Ephesians one of the seven.

It may be taken therefore as highly probable that it was the Pauline Corpus which served as the model for the letter-collections in Revelation and Ignatius, and that it was the corpus of ten letters as it is known to us, including all the Pauline epistles, apart from the Pastorals.

Goodspeed believes that the assembling of these ten letters into a corpus, and its publication, is a landmark in the story of the New Testament, and he uses vivid metaphors to convey his sense of its importance. 'The Pauline Corpus is the roof tree of the New Testament Literature. It is the watershed, the great divide, of the New Testament continent. New Testament Introduction must be rewritten in the light of it. . . . The influence of that *published* literature can be traced in document

C

after document, and they cannot be understood without the recognition of that influence' (*NC*, p. 72).

J. Knox in his study of *Marcion and the New Testament* also claims that Paul's ten letters were collected and published toward the end of the first century. He rejects Bauer's opinion that Marcion himself was 'the first systematic collector of Paul's literary remains'. Marcion simply used (and slightly rearranged) the collection of Pauline letters which he found already prepared and in use, and this had been drawn up 'early in the last decade of the first century' and 'provided both stimulus and model for subsequent Christian writing'. . . . 'That late in the first century there was a definite publication of Pauline letters has, I believe, been established with better than reasonable certainty' (*MNT*, p. 57).

It is not possible here to make a detailed examination of all the books of the New Testament to ascertain how far Goodspeed's table, quoted above, may be regarded as wholly trustworthy. Its claim, however, for Ephesians is, we believe, correct. Elsewhere[6] the present writer has tried to demonstrate that this epistle reflects acquaintance with each one of Paul's nine other epistles, to an extent and in a manner strikingly different from the natural community of thought and expression found to exist between genuinely Pauline epistles. These nine Pauline epistles must therefore have been collected, and ready for publication, if not actually published, at the time when Ephesians was written. This cannot have taken place later than A.D. 95 because other writings of that date and soon afterwards reflect an acquaintance with the phrases and ideas peculiar to Ephesians. If therefore we can claim that the Pauline Corpus came into being after Luke-Acts, but before Ephesians, we are able to bring it within a single decade. Its publication must almost certainly have taken place between A.D. 85 and 95. The evidence for this, however, is not confined to Ephesians.

P. N. Harrison has shown that the Pastoral Epistles reveal an acquaintance with Paul's letters, probably with all ten of

[6] *Epistle to the Ephesians: Its Authorship, Origin and Purpose* (Oxford University Press).

them, because they reproduce phrases from them (*PPE*, pp. 87ff). He summarizes his conclusions thus: 'These provide still clearer evidence (i.e. than Polycarp's letter) of the existence, when they were written, of all ten Paulines as a collection, almost certainly at Ephesus' (*PTE*, p. 7). This conclusion has generally commended itself to scholars. Streeter, for instance, takes it as fully proved: 'The author of the Pastorals . . . knew the ten Epistles as a collection already venerated in the Church' (*PC*, p. 160).

It is generally agreed that the author of the Fourth Gospel was probably acquainted with Paul's epistles, though it might be difficult to substantiate in its entirety Goodspeed's claim that the author of the Johannine Literature can be shown to have revealed acquaintance with all ten of the epistles. Moffatt clearly assumes some such acquaintance on the part of this author when he states that he 'has developed his theology from Pauline germs' (*ILNT*, p. 522), and this is by no means an isolated judgement. W. F. Howard in his valuable review of *The Fourth Gospel in Recent Criticism and Interpretation* gives quotations from the works of H. J. Holtzmann (p. 168), Deissmann (p. 168), B. W. Bacon (pp. 19, 44), and H. A. A. Kennedy (p. 228), which show that they also believe that this author was not only familiar with Pauline doctrines, but indebted to them. W. F. Howard himself supports, as against Schweitzer's denial, Deissmann's dictum that 'the greatest monument of the most genuine understanding of Paul's mysticism is the Gospel and Epistles of John' (pp. 168, 201). On this evidence therefore, quite apart from that provided by the study of Ephesians, the Pauline Corpus may be taken as an accomplished fact by the time that the Pastoral Epistles and the Fourth Gospel came to be written.

A great number of parallels can be drawn between Paul's epistles and 1 Peter. Those who do not feel themselves compelled to accept the Petrine origin of this epistle have interpreted these similarities as due to the author's acquaintance with the letters of Paul. Those who retain the traditional authorship are unable to do this, and explain these items of close correspondence in other ways: perhaps Peter had close associations with Paul during his final imprisonment and so became familiar with his mode of thinking and speaking; or, as Selwyn insists, they both drew on standardized church catechisms and 'household codes';[7] or, in the Thessalonian letters, it may be the association of Silvanus both with them and with 1 Peter that accounts for the similarities. We cannot pretend to decide the question of the authorship of 1 Peter here, but if it is dated, as many do date it,[8] soon after A.D. 100, it can certainly be claimed that the author's apparent knowledge of the Pauline letters points to their publication before that date.

The Second Epistle of Peter speaks of Paul by name, and deplores the perverse way in which some have so grievously misinterpreted his writings as to find in them an excuse for gross wrong-doing. The epistle refers to 'all' Paul's epistles, as though many of them were known.

The crucial evidence for Goodspeed is that afforded by Revelation. He believes it can be shown that this writing reveals acquaintance with all except two of the Pauline epistles, and since these two are 2 Corinthians and 2 Thessalonians, which were probably at that time not separate from 1 Corinthians and 1 Thessalonians, it can be taken that their omission does not imply that they were missing from the collection of letters known to the author of Revelation. The evidence, he claims, enables us to assume that all the corpus was known to this writer. Since this is probably the earliest writing after the Pauline epistles themselves and the Synoptic Gospels, it becomes important evidence for the dating of the appearance of the Pauline Corpus. If the date of Revelation is about A.D. 95 and the date of Matthew and Luke-Acts about A.D. 85, and if we assume that the Synoptic Gospels were written in complete ignorance of Paul's letters, and Revelation in full knowledge of them, here is further evidence that the corpus of these letters was published in this short interval between the two. If this claim of Goodspeed for Revelation can therefore be substantiated, it will be of vital significance. R. H.

[7] For a criticism of this explanation of these similarities, see the article in the *Journal of Theological Studies*, New Series, Vol. I, Part 1, pp. 67-73: 'The Relationship between 1 Peter and Ephesians', by C. L. Mitton.

[8] F. W. Beare in his recent commentary on 1 Peter (1947) decides in favour of a date *c*. A.D. 111-12.

Charles in Volume I of his commentary on Revelation has drawn up a careful list of correspondences between Revelation and other books of the New Testament. In so far as these concern the Pauline epistles his verdict is: 'Our author appears to have used . . . 1 Thessalonians, 1 and 2 Corinthians, Colossians, Ephesians, and possibly Galatians' (pp. lxxxiii ff). This does not corroborate the full claim of Goodspeed, but it certainly goes a long way in supporting it.

It is not, however, merely the apparent echoes of phrases and ideas from the Pauline letters which strongly suggest that the author of Revelation knew the ten collected letters, but also the very curious literary device with which the apocalypse opens. What could have led the author to preface it with a collection of letters to different churches, seven addressed to individual churches, and one, introducing the seven, addressed to all the churches collectively? It does not give the impression of being a purely spontaneous idea. In view of the probability that the Pauline Corpus included letters to seven individual churches and a general letter of introduction, can this parallelism of construction in Revelation be dismissed as a mere coincidence? 'If any literary resemblance could be more striking and massive than this, it is difficult to imagine what it would be. . . . It is most unnatural for an apocalypse to begin with a letter, still less with a corpus of letters' (Goodspeed, *INT*, pp. 211-12). Certainly it does not bear the stamp of originality; it appears rather to be a somewhat unnatural subservience to some fashion or convention. What is more likely to have exerted this strong influence than the published corpus of Pauline letters? 'The portal of the Revelation was suggested by the recent appearance of a collection of Paul's letters to the seven churches. Even the salutation of 1⁴, "Blessing to you and peace", is the characteristic Pauline salutation, unknown elsewhere in the New Testament and strange to epistolary practice' (Goodspeed, *INT*, p. 212).

Certainly no better explanation of the introduction of the curious letter corpus into Revelation has been suggested, and Streeter welcomes it as a 'brilliant suggestion that John the Seer was familiar in Ephesus with letters to the churches by another whom he regarded as an inspired prophet' (*PC*, p. 160).

CHAPTER TWO

THE CONTENTS OF THE FIRST PUBLISHED
CORPUS

THE ARGUMENT just outlined has been directed to show that it may well be true that Paul's letters did not gradually emerge in the life of the Early Church, but came into being as a collection by a deliberate act of publication, probably between A.D. 85 and 95, and that all ten Pauline letters, and not less than ten, were included in the first Corpus. Little has yet been said about the counter-suggestion that some make and press, that more than ten were included, and that the Pastorals had their place in the first known collection. Since the inclusion of thirteen letters, rather than ten, would invalidate the arguments which were used in connexion with the seven-letter corpus to be found both in Revelation and Ignatius, we must pause to examine the grounds on which it is claimed that the Pastorals must be regarded as a later addition, and not as part of the contents of the original Corpus.

They were certainly included in the list of Pauline epistles in the Muratorian Canon, and Polycarp knew them. They had, however, no place in Marcion's list. The question that has to be decided is this: does Marcion's list represent the contents of the original corpus, to which other epistles have later been added, or did Marcion deliberately omit certain epistles from the Pauline Corpus as he found it, because they did not emphasize the doctrines which he cherished?

Zahn is persuaded that Marcion found the three Pastoral epistles among the letters of Paul, but omitted them for his own purposes, because he disapproved of their contents, just as he omitted parts of Luke which did not conform to his doctrines (*Geschichte des neutestamentlichen Kanons*, I.837). Had this been so, however, Tertullian would have scathingly denounced such arbitrary action. As it is, though he accuses

Marcion of much, his accusations do not appear to include a charge of the deliberate omission of whole epistles.

Goodspeed, however, is confident that Marcion's list represents that of the first corpus, and that the Pastorals were not known in their present form until a later date.[1] In fact, he claims that one of the main purposes for which these three epistles were written (or compiled) was to counter certain heretical tendencies in the Church, included among which was Marcion's own teaching. Two passages in the Pastorals in particular support this claim. The first occurs in 2 Timothy 3[16]: 'Every scripture inspired of God is also profitable for teaching, for reproof, for correction, for instruction.' This emphatic declaration of the validity of *all* Scripture may well be directed against Marcion, who declined to recognize the Scripture of the Old Covenant as in any way authoritative for Christians, and in its place made a personal selection of Christian writings to have the status of Christian Scripture. The second is 1 Timothy 6[20], where Timothy is warned to 'turn away from the profane babblings and oppositions of the knowledge which is falsely so called, which some professing have erred concerning the faith'. This explicit condemnation of 'oppositions' especially in association with 'knowledge' ($\dot{a}\nu\tau\iota\theta\acute{e}\sigma\epsilon\iota\varsigma\ \tau\hat{\eta}\varsigma\ \psi\epsilon\upsilon\delta\omega\nu\acute{\upsilon}\mu\upsilon\upsilon\ \gamma\nu\acute{\omega}\sigma\epsilon\omega\varsigma$) is very pointed, because one of the publications of Marcion, which confirmed his reputation as a heretic, bore the title, '$\dot{a}\nu\tau\iota\theta\acute{e}\sigma\epsilon\iota\varsigma$', and his emphasis on '$\gamma\nu\hat{\omega}\sigma\iota\varsigma$' also brought him under grave suspicion. It would indeed be a very curious coincidence if this detailed warning in these precise words had been issued before Marcion began to make them notorious by the special form of his teaching. If, however, the Pastoral Epistles were issued in opposition to Marcion, that would make them of too late a date to be included in the first Corpus of Pauline letters.

W. Bauer also took this point of view. He argued that the earlier collection of ten letters had lent itself too easily to heretical interpretation in certain respects, and that the Pastorals were deliberately compiled to range Paul unmistakably on the side of ecclesiastical orthodoxy and to remove the

[1] This coincides with the opinion of Harnack, already quoted on page 19.

suspicions about Paul which were felt in some church circles.[2]

Moreover it has been demonstrated by P. N. Harrison in his book on the Pastoral Epistles that these epistles reveal an acquaintance with all the other ten Pauline epistles. This must mean that the other ten were collected and published before the three Pastorals were produced, unless indeed it could be argued for them, as Goodspeed argues for Ephesians, that they were introduced to serve as a safeguard by those who originally planned and carried out the formation of the corpus. This cannot be regarded as a probable supposition. Correctives appear later than the things they seek to correct.

One stumbling-block in the way of giving these letters a date later than A.D. 110 has been the fact that Polycarp was almost certainly acquainted with them, and Ignatius may have been. The parallels, however, with Ignatius are inconclusive, and may be explained as the result of acquaintance with Ignatius's letters on the part of the compiler of the Pastorals, or else as due to the mutual use of modes of speech which were common in the Christian communities in the early years of the second century. It is less easy to explain the much clearer parallels in Polycarp in this way, so that if Polycarp's letter is to be dated about A.D. 110, it must mean that the Pastorals had been published long enough before this time for Polycarp to become familiar with them. Even this would allow time for them to be produced later than the original corpus, but not very much time. And in any case there are other reasons for thinking that a later date should be accorded to them. This dilemma seems to have been the clue which led to the detailed study of Polycarp's letter by P. N. Harrison. His conclusion is that this letter is in reality two letters, written at different times, but later combined into one. The shorter one, consisting of paragraphs xiii and xiv, he calls the 'Covering Letter', which was sent to the Philippian Church in company with the letters of Ignatius. The longer one, paragraphs i-xii, he names the 'Crisis Letter', and for this a date as late even as A.D. 140 may

---

[2] W. Bauer in *Rechtgläubigkeit und Ketzerei in ältesten Christentum*, p. 228: '*Von hier aus möchte ich die Pastoralbriefe verstehen als einen Versuch der Kirche, Paulus unmissverständlich in die antihäretische Front einzugliedern und den Mangel an Vertrauen zu ihm in Kirchlichen Kreisen zu beheben.*'

be appropriate. It is significant that it is in this longer and later letter that the similarities with the Pastoral Epistles are found. If these conclusions are correct, it means that there is no evidence which compels us to date the Pastorals earlier than the third, or even the fourth, decade of the second century.

J. Knox also, in his study of *Marcion and the New Testament*, contends that Marcion's collection of ten Pauline epistles is identical with the collection which formed the original corpus, and that the Pastorals came to be added later, and were not, as Zahn and others argued, omitted by Marcion. The grounds for his opinion are substantially the same as those outlined above: that all ten of these letters can be shown to have influenced *1 Clement*, Ignatius, and Polycarp; that the group of letters in Revelation and the speed with which the letters of Ignatius were assembled suggest that in each case a prototype is being followed, and that this prototype is the Pauline Corpus of ten letters, rather than one consisting of thirteen letters; and that 'there is almost irrefutable evidence for the dating of the three Pastoral Epistles well into the second century—which means that if there was a publication of a Pauline collection before A.D. 100, it cannot have contained these letters' (*MNT*, p. 58).

We take it therefore as highly probable, if not actually certain, that the Pauline Corpus as first published about A.D. 90 contained only ten letters, and not the thirteen which were included in it later.

There is a curious sentence in the letter of Ignatius to Ephesus which has a bearing on the contents of the early Pauline Corpus. Unfortunately its meaning is most obscure, and its significance for this inquiry cannot be determined with any degree of confidence. The sentence occurs in Ignatius's epistle to the Ephesians, 12². There Paul is referred to as one 'ὃς ἐν πάσῃ ἐπιστολῇ μνημονεύει ὑμῶν ἐν Χριστῷ Ἰησοῦ.'. The word πᾶς, used without the article, means 'every',[3] and explanations which resort to some other meaning, such as 'in the whole letter', must be rejected. The sentence, therefore,

---

[3] C. F. D. Moule in *An Idiom Book of New Testament Greek*, pp. 94-5, quotes instances which may be exceptions to this rule.

must mean: 'He remembers you' (or 'makes mention of you') 'in every letter'. Some have been content to dismiss the difficulty as arising from a pardonable overstatement which should not be pressed. But this is probably to take the matter too lightly. In Paul's genuine letters there is only one reference to Ephesus, and that is in 1 Corinthians. Three others occur in the Pastoral Epistles. It may be argued that 'Ephesians' itself should be added, though no reference to Ephesus appears in its original text, and we do not know that this title had come to be associated with the letter as early as the time of Ignatius. Some also claim that Romans 16 was originally a brief letter to the church at Ephesus, and therefore should count as a 'mention' of Ephesus. It is, however, unlikely that either Ignatius or his readers would have the means of reaching such a conclusion. If we were able to count the Pastoral Epistles among the original collection, we might accept Ignatius's statement as an excusable exaggeration, arising from a desire to compliment the Ephesian church, and from a superficial acquaintance with Paul's letters. 'But if the Pastorals were not included in his collection of the letters of Paul, 1 Corinthians would remain as the only letter in which Ephesus is even named' (Streeter, PC, p. 102). For this reason Streeter is inclined to think that the Pastorals must have been included in Ignatius's collection of the Pauline epistles, though not necessarily in the original collection.

P. N. Harrison (PTE, p. 250) cannot accept this early date for the Pastorals and explains Ignatius's sentence as justified on four grounds: (1) He had long known 1 Corinthians, so that its one reference to Ephesus loomed large in his memory. (2) He knew 'Ephesians' in a copy which had the name of the church inserted in the opening verse. (3) He knew enough about the local circumstances of the Ephesian church to be aware that Romans 16, with 'its crowded references to Paul's friends at Ephesus', was addressed to Ephesus. (4) 'He had also been shown (either by Polycarp or by the delegates from Ephesus) that little bundle of three short notes addressed by the Apostle to Timothy at Ephesus on various occasions, including his Last Letter.' It was these 'short notes' which were later incorporated into the Pastorals.

None of these explanations of Ignatius's overstatement is convincing. Goodspeed is therefore quite justified in attempting a new line of elucidation. He suggests that Ignatius is, in this sentence, paying the Ephesian church a delicate compliment, which they at any rate would at once appreciate, because it is a charming acknowledgement of the part they had played in assembling the Pauline Corpus. It is a recognition of the fact that it was at Ephesus, and through the agency of some leader in the Ephesian church, that Paul's letters had first been brought together and issued as a collection. In this sense it was true that every letter in the collection was a reminder of the church which had rescued Paul's letters from oblivion and made them known to the whole community of believers. P. N. Harrison agrees that 'this avoids the difficulties inherent in other theories', but adds a caution: 'But will the words of Ignatius bear this meaning?' (*PTE*, p. 249).

It depends on the meaning which can be assigned to μνημονεύω. In the New Testament it is used only once with the meaning 'to make mention of' (He 11^{22}), and there it is followed by the preposition περί with the genitive. Normally, and elsewhere in the New Testament, it means 'to bear in mind' or 'to call to mind', but in the sense of remembering something oneself, not of reminding someone else. But it is this meaning of 'bringing something to someone else's mind' which is required by Goodspeed's solution. No instance of this use of the word appears in the New Testament, but Liddell and Scott in their lexicon give one or two instances of it, so that Goodspeed's interpretation cannot be rejected on the ground of attributing an impossible meaning to the word. The use of the word in Hebrews 11^{22} might also be claimed as a parallel, since there the word might be translated, 'drew their attention to', though, as we noticed above, it is there used with a preposition and not with a simple genitive.

Goodspeed's suggested solution does not immediately win one's judgement, but there is no insuperable objection to it.

CHAPTER THREE

THE PLACE OF THE ORIGIN OF THE PAULINE CORPUS

EVEN IF WE are not able to accept Goodspeed's explanation of this perplexing sentence from Ignatius, and see in it evidence that Ephesian Christians initiated the collection and publication of Paul's letters, there are other grounds for associating their first appearance with the district of Ephesus.

We saw that Harnack disclaimed any conviction on this issue, and confessed: 'It is no longer possible to discover where the great final collection took place' (*ONT*, p. 27), but his opinion, and Zahn's also, inclined to give the credit to Corinth. P. N. Harrison follows their lead, and recapitulates the arguments used by Harnack in its favour as follows (*PTE*, pp. 236ff): 1 Corinthians stood first in the earliest collection, and because of this position had its original opening greeting amplified, so that it ceased to be addressed to an individual church, though such an address is required by the whole character of the epistle, and included, besides the Corinthian Christians, 'all that call upon the name of the Lord Jesus in every place' (1 Co 1²). This modification was made only because 1 Corinthians introduced the whole corpus. But the fact of its being given this place of prominence points to Corinth as the place where the letters were first brought together. There is also the well-known editorial process which combined perhaps four separate letters, or parts of letters, into the two letters which we now know as 1 and 2 Corinthians. This process is also held to indicate a Corinthian origin for the collection. In addition, Harrison claims that 'the central position of Corinth' and 'its activity and vitality' support the hypothesis.

One feels that these are not very strong arguments on which to base a confident preference for Corinth, and J. Knox has little difficulty in countering them in favour of Ephesus (*MNT*,

pp. 174-5). Quite apart from the arguments that suggest that
Ephesians originally held the place of honour at the forefront
of the corpus, the prominent position accorded to the Corinthian correspondence is probably due to no other consideration
than its length. If our two letters to Corinth were treated as
one unit, they would be by far the longest unit in the collection.
The editorial process which modified its opening address to
make it applicable to a wider audience than that originally
intended, and combined several letters into two units (or
possibly one long unit which was only later sub-divided), need
nŏt be located at Corinth. Precisely the same thing might
have happened wherever and whenever the scattered individual letters were brought together and arranged for publication. Nor is Corinth's centrality and activity positive evidence
in its favour. From what we know, Ephesus was not much less
central, and certainly not less active. Harrison's theory,
though mainly favourable to Corinth, is not unaware of the
claims of Ephesus, and allows that the work, begun at Corinth,
may have been brought to its final form at Ephesus. Knox,
however, finds the claim for Corinth in this respect, whether
in whole or in part, unconvincing.

Certainly Ephesus was just the place where one might have
expected such an enterprise to be undertaken and carried to
completion. Harnack called it the 'second fulcrum of Christianity' after Antioch. It played a large part in Paul's ministry.
He remained there for the unusually long period of three
years. His correspondence with Corinth dates from that
period, and probably several others of his letters as well. The
city is given great prominence in Acts. Such important names
as Apollos, Aquila and Priscilla are associated with it. A
unique honour is accorded to it in the description of its elders
being summoned to Miletus to meet Paul for a final leave-
taking and to hear a last message from him. Romans 16
seems to have been written for a Christian woman of Cenchrea
to introduce her to the Christians at Ephesus. Revelation was
written in that part of Asia Minor, and so also was the Fourth
Gospel and the rest of the Johannine Literature. Ignatius
addressed one of his seven letters to Ephesus. Some claim that
Luke-Acts came into being there, and though this is far from

proved, if it were true it would provide an explanation for the great prominence of Ephesus in Acts. Thus a large proportion of the New Testament is linked in one way or another with this city. Moreover we know that the coast towns of Asia Minor were centres of literary activity. It was at Pergamum, not many miles to the north, that parchment was first produced to replace papyrus, when this customary material for writing became almost unprocurable in Asia. The demand of the publishing activities of the area led to the creation of this new commodity to supply their needs.

In addition to the general suitability of Ephesus for sponsoring a literary event of such importance there are several other good reasons for associating this first Pauline Corpus with Ephesus. These reasons are presented by Goodspeed, with his customary vigour, in several of his books. A summary of them may be found in his *Introduction to the New Testament* (pp. 217-19). In marshalling his arguments he assumes the accuracy of his theory of the origin of Ephesians, and those who do not accept that theory will find this a weak point in his case. His main arguments are as follows:

(1) The nucleus of the collection of Paul's letters lay in the association of Colossians and the other letter referred to in Colossians 4[16]. Goodspeed believes this other letter to have been what we know today as the Epistle to Philemon. It is on Paul's explicit instructions (Col 4[16]) that these letters are brought together, and that each of them is read to two separate Christian congregations. Since they were both addressed to churches in Asia Minor, it is probable that someone in that area who had knowledge of these two would proceed from this beginning to acquire others as he came to know of them.

(2) If 'Ephesians' is accepted as the collector's own introduction to the corpus, being itself a recapitulation of the main doctrines contained in the other letters, its predominant dependence on Colossians suggests that its author was one who had known Colossians far longer and more intimately than the others. That would be true only of one who had lived in that area of Asia Minor.

(3) It is in Revelation that we find the first unmistakable

acquaintance with the whole Pauline Corpus. Since Revelation is a product of the area of Ephesus, and it would be natural to expect the first reflection of the published corpus to appear in the area where it first became known, this too points to Ephesus.

(4) It was in the neighbourhood of Ephesus that Ignatius conceived the idea of writing a group of seven letters, probably because he had recently become acquainted with the similar collection of Paul's.

(5) The great influence of Paul's letters on the Johannine writings is best understood if these letters had long been familiar in the neighbourhood of Ephesus, where the Fourth Gospel was produced.

(6) Many critics have felt that Romans 16 was originally a separate letter to Ephesus. But how could its incorporation within the Epistle to the Romans be explained? P. N. Harrison suggests that when Paul sent this private note to Ephesus he also sent a copy of Romans along with it, so that at Ephesus the two were from the first attached to each other. Even if this were so, it would mark Ephesus as the place where Romans, at any rate, was first given its place in the Corpus. Otherwise Romans would not have become known in this longer form which incorporated what was originally a separate note to Ephesus. Goodspeed, however, sees this association of the two letters as due to the editor rather than to Paul himself. He suggests that the editor had this small private note before him. It had been preserved at Ephesus as a souvenir of Paul, and he wanted to find a place for it in the collection, though it was hardly suitable to stand there alone, in its own right, since it was little more than a list of names. He attached it, therefore, to the last chapter of Romans, where it could stand quite unobtrusively. But if it had not been at Ephesus where this editor was working, this Ephesian fragment would hardly have come to his notice or have seemed worthy of incorporation.

(7) Goodspeed also uses his interpretation of Ignatius's remark to the Ephesian church that in every letter Paul 'mentions' them, or 'brings them to mind'. As we have seen, Goodspeed explains this as a courteous word of congratulation

on the part they have taken in publishing the whole collection of Paul's letters. 'The Ephesians would understand the gracious allusion' (*INT*, p. 219).

Both B. H. Streeter and J. Knox agree with Goodspeed in recognizing Ephesus as the place of origin of the Pauline Corpus. Knox adds other arguments to those put forward by Goodspeed. In *Philemon among the Letters of Paul* he stresses how inappropriate it was that the Epistle to Philemon should have found a place in the canon of Christian Scriptures. So brief and private a letter seems to have no claim to such status. Nor is this only a modern fancy. Jerome says that many contemporaries of his objected to it as trivial compared with the other letters. Tertullian too speaks of it disparagingly in comparison with the other personal letters in the collection, that is the three Pastorals. Yet in the earliest collection these three were not present to obscure the great difference in length between Philemon and the Church letters. Why was it included at all? There must be some specially important reason. Knox emphasizes this: 'The more anomalous the presence of Philemon in the collection appears, the more significant it must be. The more grounds which can be cited for its exclusion, the more important must have been the ground upon which it was actually included. The very fact that Philemon seems so out of place is evidence that the original editors had very good reason for including it. We are convinced that if we knew that reason we should know something very important about the publication of the Pauline letters' (*PLP*, p. 46). Its close link with Colossians would facilitate its acceptance, but not wholly explain it, because it never lost its identity as a separate letter. Its very presence in the corpus suggests that the collector must have had strong personal reasons for its inclusion. These personal reasons very probably include a long personal acquaintance with it, and since the letter was directed to the neighbourhood of Colossæ, such a long personal acquaintance would imply that the collector himself was associated with that district of Asia Minor of which Ephesus was the metropolis.

Knox also brings into the argument the Marcionite Prologues to the Letters of Paul (*MNT*, pp. 169-70). In them

Ephesus is named as the place of origin of Galatians, Colossians, and the Corinthian letters. This is in excess of what tradition has usually ascribed to Ephesus, and Knox claims that it 'may be cited as evidence of an early tradition associating Paul's letters as a whole with that city' (*MNT*, p. 175).

D

CHAPTER FOUR

THE COLLECTOR OF THE PAULINE CORPUS

IT IS ONLY to be expected that when these conclusions have been reached about the formation of the Pauline Corpus, and the date and place of its first appearance approximately fixed, the further question should be raised: 'Can the collector be identified with any known figure in the early Church?'

Evidence has been given for locating the origin of this corpus in the area of Ephesus, and dating it between the publication of Luke-Acts and the writing of Revelation, that is about A.D. 90. There is also a high degree of probability that the surprising inclusion of Philemon points to some personal link between the collector and this letter. The very presence of this letter which deals with so personal an issue might well, of itself, be sufficient to raise the inquiry whether any of the people mentioned in it could possibly have been the collector—Philemon himself, or Archippus, or Onesimus. Is there any reason to believe that any one of these was alive and prominent thirty years after Paul's death? Or even if they were still living, is there any reason to think that any of them was the kind of person who would be capable of carrying through such an enterprise? Moreover, if Goodspeed is right in identifying the collector with the writer of Ephesians, we should have to ask further whether any of them was likely to be capable of so fine a literary achievement.

The only name of these three which reappears in the neighbourhood of Ephesus in the later years of the first century is that of Onesimus. The Bishop of Ephesus at the time of Ignatius's stay in Asia Minor bore that name. If there was any possibility that the runaway slave might be the same man as the Bishop, he would seem a very likely candidate for this honour of having reintroduced Paul through his letters to a generation that was becoming forgetful of him. Goodspeed is clearly attracted to this possibility, but he tries to preserve an attitude of judicial caution in his comment: 'This is all in the realm of conjecture, it is true, but it has no small degree of probability' (*CP*, p. 58).

J. Knox, in his book on *Philemon among the Letters of Paul*, has carried the matter farther. He elaborates the arguments noted above, and then in Chapter 5 produces impressive evidence for identifying Bishop Onesimus of Ephesus, to whom Ignatius refers in terms of deep respect in the letter he writes to Ephesus, with Onesimus, the runaway slave, for whom Paul pleads in his letter to Philemon. This evidence consists of a detailed examination of the language of Ignatius's letter. He is able to show that this letter includes a remarkable number of similarities with Paul's letter to Philemon, for which it is very difficult to account, except on the assumption that Ignatius is playfully quoting from memory certain phrases from it. But there would be little point in such an indirect appeal to the words and thoughts of Paul's letter, unless the Bishop were indeed the same man as the slave of that name.

Ignatius would find it appropriate enough to appeal to this earlier letter of Paul, because there is a superficial resemblance between the circumstances in which he is writing, and those in which Paul wrote. Both writers are asking, as a favour, that someone may be released from present obligations so as to give attendance to the writer. Ignatius's request is that two of the deputation from Ephesus may be allowed to remain with him, instead of returning immediately to their duties at Ephesus. The passages which bear the closest resemblance to each other are quoted below, and the corresponding words and phrases are underlined and marked with corresponding signs:

Ignatius ad Eph. ii	*Philemon 13*
περὶ δὲ τοῦ συνδούλου μου Βούρρου τοῦ κατὰ θεὸν διακόνου* ὑμῶν ἐν πᾶσιν εὐλογημένου, εὔχομαι** παραμεῖναι† αὐτὸν εἰς τιμὴν ὑμῶν†† καὶ τοῦ ἐπισκόπου.	ὃν ἐγὼ ἐβουλόμην** πρὸς ἐμαυτὸν κατέχειν† ἵνα ὑπὲρ σοῦ†† μοι διακονῇ* ἐν τοῖς δεσμοῖς τοῦ εὐαγγελίου.

It would be unusual for four such points of similarity to appear within so short a space entirely by coincidence. Nor are these all. Chapter 2 of Ignatius's letter to the Ephesians is a very short chapter consisting of only fifteen lines, but there occur in it, in addition to those words marked in the above quotation, two other words that also occur in Philemon: ἀνέπαυσεν ('refreshed') (Phlm. 7 and 20) and ὀναίμην ('let me have joy') (Phlm. 20).

A still more impressive sequence of resemblances is indicated by Knox in Chapter 3 of Ignatius's letter:

Ignatius ad Eph. iii	*Philemon 8-9*
οὐ διατάσσομαι* ὑμῖν ὡς ὧν τις** εἰ γὰρ καὶ δέδεμαι*** ἐν τῷ ὀνόματι, οὔπω ἀπήρτισμαι . . ἀλλὰ ἐπεὶ ἡ ἀγάπη† οὐκ ἐᾷ με σιωπᾶν περὶ ὑμῶν, διὰ τοῦτο† προέλαβον παρακαλεῖν†† ὑμᾶς.	διὸ, πολλὴν · ἐν Χριστῷ παρρησίαν ἔχων ἐπιτάσσειν* σοι τὸ ἀνῆκον, διὰ τὴν ἀγάπην† μᾶλλον παρακαλῶ,†† τοιοῦτος ὢν ὡς Παῦλος πρεσβύτης,** νυνὶ δὲ καὶ δέσμιος*** Χριστοῦ Ἰησοῦ.

(An English translation of these passages is given in an appendix on page 77).

There are further similarities also which Knox points out. Cumulatively they make it difficult to avoid the conclusion that Ignatius is deliberately following the line of appeal which Paul had taken in his letter to Philemon. This is the more remarkable because elsewhere Philemon is not reflected in the letters of Ignatius, nor indeed in any of the writings of the second century. It does seem as though some special reason induced Ignatius to draw upon it in this particular letter. The first six chapters of the letter are, in effect, addressed to the Bishop of the church at Ephesus, rather than to the whole church and it is in these chapters that all the resemblances to Philemon occur. In view of this, is it a mere coincidence that the Bishop's name happens to be Onesimus? Knox thinks that more than a coincidence is involved. He argues further that the phrasing in Paul's letter to Philemon implies a request not only that Onesimus should be set free, but that he should also be sent back to Paul to be his personal helper; that Paul was probably in Ephesus when this request was sent, temporarily in prison, but expecting release soon; that the request was almost certainly granted, otherwise the letter would not have survived; that it would therefore be to Ephesus that Onesimus would go with his newly-granted freedom; and that there he would, under Paul's direction, take up his work as a Christian. He must have been a person of unusual promise for Paul to make so special a plea on his behalf, and to seek not only his pardon but also his release from slavery in order that he might become Paul's colleague in the work of the Gospel. In the subsequent appointment of Bishops, an intimate acquaintance with an apostle would almost certainly be counted a high qualification for the post.

Such are the arguments which have been used to support the proposed identification of the collector of the Pauline Corpus (and the writer of Ephesians) with Onesimus, the one-time slave.

Others have wondered if Tychicus might have been the author of Ephesians. This would certainly offer an explanation for the inclusion at Eph 6^{21-2} of the long passage from Colossians about Tychicus. W. L. Knox, for instance, writes: 'The allusion to Tychicus may be a thinly veiled statement of the author's identity' (*PCG*, p. 203). Moffatt, however, interprets the purpose behind the inclusion of this passage as being merely 'to lend "*vraisemblance*" to the writing' (*ILNT*, p. 393). Alternatively, it may be, even if Onesimus or some other actually carried through the collecting of the epistles and the compiling of the introduction to them, that Tychicus was still living, and was closely associated with the enterprise, and that this is a courteous acknowledgement of his encouragement and support.

At any rate this can be said: if it was Onesimus who made the collection of Paul's letters (and also compiled Ephesians), it does at any rate provide a satisfactory explanation for the inclusion of Philemon in the corpus, and for the predominant influence of Colossians in the composition of Ephesians.

This attempt, however, to identify the unknown collector (whether or not he be also author of Ephesians), though full of interest, is exceedingly speculative, and in any case is not in itself a matter of importance.

CHAPTER FIVE

THE OCCASION OF THE FORMATION OF THE PAULINE CORPUS

GOODSPEED, as we have seen, believes that the formation of this Corpus can be dated between the publication of Luke-Acts and the writing of Revelation, because the former shows no knowledge of the ten letters, and the latter apparently knows all of them. He also believes that a still closer relationship than this exists between Acts and the Pauline Corpus; for it was the publication of Acts, he claims, which implanted the idea of collecting Paul's letters in some fertile mind. He pictures some unknown Asian Christian, who has long treasured the two letters of Paul which he has known intimately for many years, Colossians and Philemon, but who is unaware that any similar letters had been written to other churches. To him Paul is a supremely great figure whom he cannot forget. But a new generation is growing up to whom Paul is just a name which the older Christians mention with veneration from time to time, and even these older people speak of him less frequently than once they did. Then Acts is published, with its vivid stirring narrative. Every Christian who can read is soon familiar with its story, and those who cannot read hear it from those who can. At once Paul becomes a living figure, even to those who have never seen him. He is no longer just a name, but a name wonderfully enriched by this exciting portrait of a most gallant and enterprising apostle of the early Church. Paul becomes immediately the centre of a new spate of interest, and everyone wants to know still more about him. Questions are asked: Did he write any books or leave any written record of his addresses? Can anything more be added to what is recorded in Acts? One alert reader knows at least of two letters which Paul wrote, and his mind is beginning to probe into further possibilities: if Paul wrote these two, is it not likely that he wrote others? if the church

at Colossæ received one, would not some other churches have
been equally fortunate? If, previously, ignorance concerning
which other churches might be most usefully approached had
restrained this disciple from inquiry, Acts now remedied that
ignorance. It contained many names of churches where Paul
had worked. He could inquire of these. In his most hopeful
moments he could never have anticipated so rich a response
to his search. The churches of Galatia, Philippi, Thessalonica,
Corinth and Rome all had in their church chests correspondence from Paul. He was able to make his own copy of each,
and at last had in his hands his precious treasury of six
separate groups of Paul's letters. It is worth noting that for
one who already knew of the letters to the Colossians and to
Philemon, Acts would serve as a guide to all the others. But it
would not have led any investigator to the places where these
two could have been found, for Colossæ and Laodicea are not
mentioned in Acts. These newly collected letters were then
published as a corpus, just at the moment when the minds of
Christians everywhere were most ready to give them a welcome
and to appreciate them.

Streeter reports this suggested relationship of cause and
effect between Acts and the Pauline Corpus, and gives it his
approval (*PC*, p. 159). He also agrees with Goodspeed in
attaching the utmost importance to the appearance of these
collected letters, since together they are of immensely greater
value than when they were simply isolated units, however
influential they may have been in their own area. W. L.
Knox, however, while acknowledging that Goodspeed's theory
'appears to offer a convincing solution both of the authorship
of Ephesians, and of its great value and importance as a
statement of Paulinism' is not 'clear that it is necessary to
suppose . . . that the author wrote after the publication of
Luke-Acts' (*PCG*, p. 184). J. Knox, too, though he is persuaded of the accuracy of Goodspeed's theory in nearly every
other particular, dissents at this point, because he believes that
Acts in its present form was not published till nearly the
middle of the second century and that part at any rate of its
purpose was to counter the heretical tendencies fostered by
Marcion (*MNT*, pp. 139, 173).

It may be that the final form of Acts was not fixed until well on in the second century, but the consensus of opinion is that Luke-Acts in substantially its present form was published before A.D. 90. Goodspeed's theory does not insist that the first stimulating issue of Acts was in all respects identical with the final form in which it was preserved by the Church, but that the main story of Acts became known soon after A.D. 85. This item in Goodspeed's theory seems very probable, quite apart from any bearing it may have had upon the production of Ephesians.

Those, however, who favour the identification of the collector of the letters with Onesimus, may argue that one so intimately connected with Paul in his work would not need the information which is provided in Acts to direct him to the churches where Paul had done his chief work. It may well have been, however, that his own deep loyalty to Paul was established in a new confidence by this record in Acts of his heroic witness to the faith, so that he was stimulated to this new venture which previously might have seemed hardly worth while. Moreover, the attitude of the ordinary Christian to Paul was changed by the influence of Acts. However indifferent he may have been to him previously, he was now ready to receive with avidity and veneration whatever bore his name and authority. So, even if Acts did not provide this potential collector with information which he had earlier lacked, it did present his devotion to Paul with a great stimulus, and an atmosphere in which it could work with remarkable effectiveness. Acts, therefore, may have played a decisive part in prompting this enterprise of loyalty to a revered master, by which both the memory of Paul was served and the literature of the Church immeasurably enriched, even though that part is not exactly the one which Goodspeed accords to it.[1]

[1] In my book on *The Epistle to the Ephesians* (pp. 273-6), I argued that part of the purpose of the epistle was to reintroduce the Gospel of Jesus Christ as Paul had understood and expounded it, the Gospel of the Free Grace of God apprehended by Faith, to a generation which was already slipping back toward a moralistic interpretation of the Christian message as a way of life by which man may find favour with God. If this was true of the origin of 'Ephesians', the same motive, in part at any rate, may have actuated the man who first collected Paul's genuine letters, and made them available to the whole Church.

CHAPTER SIX

THE PUBLICATION OF THE CORPUS

THERE MAY be those who hesitate about the use of the word 'publication' in connexion with Christian literature before the end of the first century. Is it true to say that the Pauline Corpus was 'published'? Was such a thing even possible among the Christians at that early date? Would it not rather be a case of one individual laboriously making a private copy of another individual's manuscript?

Certainly Cicero published collections of his letters, and so did the younger Pliny, and among the Greeks there were collected letters of Plato and Apollonius. Among both Romans and Greeks publishing was a highly organized business. Large numbers of educated slaves were employed to copy simultaneously what one reader dictated. In this way a great many copies were produced at the same time, and much more quickly than it would have taken one solitary individual to make one copy, unaided by a reader. Is it legitimate, however, to imagine anything comparable to this being done for Christian books before the end of the first century?

We have been so deeply impressed by Paul's description of the Christians at Corinth as a somewhat mean, uncultured company, including 'not many wise after the flesh, not many mighty, not many noble' (1 Co 1²⁶), that we have failed to do justice to the vigour, ingenuity and ability of the Christians of a later generation. After all, thirty years of Christian living can work a great transformation, and in any case it does not necessarily follow that those who responded to the Christian message at Ephesus were so uninfluential and uneducated as those at Corinth had been. Recent discoveries of early Christian literature are compelling us to revise our earlier preconceptions, for these discoveries make us aware of an unexpected spirit of enterprise and initiative among the early Christians in the production and publication of literary works.

For instance, we tended to take it for granted that all Christian writings would be produced on rolls, in the old-fashioned way, for the first few centuries. Even if prosperous commercial firms could venture upon the new-fangled codex form, the poor, ignorant Christian community would have to be content with the old and familiar and obvious. But this is very far from what actually happened. In 1932 F. G. Kenyon (*RD*, p. 55) acknowledged the possibility that the Gospels were published in codex form as early as the second century. Since 1932 this possibility has been transformed into almost a certainty. In his book *Christianity goes to Press* Goodspeed summarizes the relevant discoveries which have led to this change of opinion and quotes F. G. Kenyon as saying in 1937: 'It seems that this [the papyrus codex form], if not actually the invention of the Christian community, was at any rate mainly employed by them, for, whereas the roll continued in practically universal use for works of pagan literature all through the second and third centuries, the majority of Christian works are in the codex form' (*CP*, pp. 70-1). Goodspeed also quotes other authorities who bear out this judgement of Kenyon. H. A. Sanders even goes so far as to say that 'for Christian literature, codices were probably used from the first'. That may be an overstatement, but it is probable that the Christians were pioneers in methods of publishing, and saw the possibilities of the codex and availed themselves of it more quickly than others, even if they did not actually invent it.

It would probably be an error to visualize the first issue of the Pauline Corpus, as early as A.D. 90, in codex form. Until further evidence is produced we shall be wise to assume that it appeared in roll-form. But even then it could be published. There is no reason for doubting that copies of this corpus would be produced by a large number of copyists, simultaneously writing to the dictation of one reader. Whether they were volunteers or paid servants makes no difference to the fact of publication. It means that large numbers of copies would be available as soon as one was ready.

The codex form would be needed from the first for any publication of the four Gospels as a single unit. It is doubtful if they would ever have obtained their commanding position as 'The Four', as Irenaeus knew them, had they not been capable of being published as a unit. It is very probable also that by the time of Marcion the codex was in use for the Pauline epistles, at any rate in some areas. It would have been difficult to establish a clear-cut canon, as Marcion apparently succeeded in doing, unless what was within the canon could be published as a unit, distinct from other claimants. Marcion's success in making clear his idea of the Christian canon of Scripture almost certainly points to the fact that his collection of Paul's letters, and also his version of Luke's Gospel, were bound together into one book.

This claim for the use by Christians of the codex as early as the opening decades of the first century might have seemed quite extravagant twenty years ago, but the publication of the Chester Beatty Papyri (1933-6) and of the John Rylands fragment of St John's Gospel (1935) have shown it to be well within the range of what is possible; for both these papyri were bound in the codex form, and the date of the Chester Beatty Papyri is thought to be about A.D. 200 and that of the Rylands Fragment perhaps as early as A.D. 150.

CHAPTER SEVEN

THE PLACE OF EPHESIANS IN THE PAULINE CORPUS

W E HAVE seen that good reasons can be given for believing that the Pauline letters were first collected about A.D. 90 and were published in the neighbourhood of Ephesus, probably by one who was himself intimately associated with that area.

Of all the epistles included in this original corpus, the Epistle to the Ephesians is the only one whose Pauline authorship is seriously doubted, and its inclusion in the first collection of Pauline letters is a very strong argument for its authenticity. Those who reject its Pauline authorship must provide a satisfactory explanation for its immediate and unchallenged acceptance into the corpus of Pauline letters from the very earliest times.

It is to meet this situation that Goodspeed, following up passing suggestions by J. Weiss and Jülicher, has elaborated the theory that the Epistle to the Ephesians was written, probably by the original collector of the letters, to serve as an Introduction to the Corpus. This would certainly account for its presence in the Corpus, and many of the features of the epistle accord with such an interpretation. For instance, the epistle as a whole is an admirable summary of Pauline teaching as it is known to us in the other epistles. It reveals an acquaintance with them, and has been, not inaptly, described as 'a mosaic of Pauline materials',[1] borrowed from the genuine epistles and skilfully blended together. In it Pauline ideas which in the other letters are expounded in relation to local situations and problems of the past are re-stated in general terms so as to be relevant to the whole company of believers. Some passages read like deliberate summaries of Paul's teaching on certain important aspects of the Christian Faith, e.g.

[1] Goodspeed, *ME*, p. 8.

2^{8-9} on Salvation, and 4^{4-6} on Christian Unity. The whole epistle provides Pauline theology and moral teaching with an expression admirably suited to liturgical purposes.

Indeed, if anyone had decided to take in hand the writing of an introduction to the collected Pauline epistles, with the aim of presenting the main features of Pauline thought in a form suitable for general readers and for use in public worship, this epistle is the kind of writing which might well have been produced.[2] If it were included as an 'Introduction', however, it would certainly have stood first in the original corpus. We do not know of any list in which Ephesians is given this status, but is there any evidence that perhaps at one time it did hold this honoured position? Have any traces survived? Or can we suggest any reasons why it should ever have been removed from this position, if once it held it?

Some pieces of evidence have been produced in favour of this claim on behalf of Ephesians, and these will now be stated and considered.

The order of Paul's letters in the English New Testament is not the order of the original Pauline Corpus. We have seen that it is most unlikely that the Pastorals had any place in the earliest collection of letters, and that the order in which the others were known in the second century seems to have varied. Some argue that this variation springs from the fact that several different areas made their own collections of the letters and followed their own arrangement. But if these letters were rescued from obscurity by one inspired collector and made known to the Church by one deliberate act of publication, one would expect that some trace of the original order would survive, and that explanations could be found for any later deviations from it.

The length of the epistles seems to have influenced their order from the first. In our present New Testament, apart from one small exception, the sequence runs smoothly from the longest to the shortest. This is immediately evident when the number of pages (in Westcott and Hort's *Greek Testament*) covered by each epistle is noted: Romans 26, 1 Corinthians 24,
Corinthians $16\frac{1}{2}$, Galatians $8\frac{1}{4}$, Ephesians $8\frac{3}{4}$, Philippians 6,

See Mitton, *EP*, pp. 266ff.

Colossians 6, 1 Thessalonians $5\frac{1}{2}$, 2 Thessalonians 3, and Philemon $1\frac{1}{4}$. Ephesians is the only one which breaks the orderly progression. But this in itself is of little significance because this order is not claimed as the original order, though it is highly probable that the length of the epistles was from the first a determining factor in allocating their order.

The earliest list of the contents of the Pauline Corpus which is known to us is that used by Marcion, and happily we know, not only its contents, but also the order in which the epistles are arranged. Charteris, in *Canonicity* on page 242, quotes Epiphanius (*Haeres* xlii) as listing the Pauline epistles as used by Marcion in the following order: Galatians, 1 and 2 Corinthians, Romans, 1 and 2 Thessalonians, Ephesians, Colossians, Philemon, and Philippians. The accuracy of this statement from Epiphanius is confirmed by the acceptance of the same order of the letters in Tertullian's criticism of Marcion's use of them. The only difference is that Tertullian seems to treat Philemon as though it followed Philippians and so stood last in the Corpus.

J. Knox is convinced that, in Marcion's copy of the collected letters, the two letters to Corinth were treated as a single unit, and so also the two to Thessalonica. He points out that the Marcionite prologues (which he takes to be almost contemporary with Marcion, if not actually genuine) apparently have no knowledge of any sub-division within the Corinthian and Thessalonian correspondence (*MNT*, p. 44). In support of this claim, he demonstrates at length that the opening sentences of 2 Corinthians, with their description of the writer and of the recipients and the wording of the greeting, are identical with those of 1 Corinthians, and similarly the opening sentences of 2 Thessalonians correspond almost exactly with those of 1 Thessalonians. This is remarkable, because Paul's letters generally show a considerable divergence in matters of detail in their opening sentences. Nor is there any reason why two should be identical because they happen to be addressed to the same community. Even if the description of the recipients might happen to be the same, the other parts would differ in detail, just as the letters to other communities differ. Knox explains this close correspondence by claiming that in Marcion's collection 1 and 2 Corinthians were written as one group of correspondence, with the introductory greetings omitted from all except the one letter which stood first. Later, however, when this correspondence was sub-divided, need was felt for an opening greeting to the second letter, and so the one from the first letter was copied verbatim. The same would apply to the two letters to Thessalonica (*MNT*, pp. 64-7).

Knox also believes that Philemon was similarly joined on to Colossians and the two treated as a single unit of correspondence. For this reason he accepts Epiphanius's order as opposed to Tertullian's, and believes that the two were known under the double title: 'To the Colossians and Laodiceans.' Goodspeed on the other hand thinks that Philemon stood on its own and was separately known as 'The Epistle to the Laodiceans', until Marcion gave that title to the unaddressed letter which we know as Ephesians, and so had to find another name for the smaller letter. It came to be called 'The Epistle to Philemon'—although it is addressed to two others as well—and that is the name by which it has been known ever since.

It is of course true that Marcion knew Ephesians under the title of 'The Epistle to the Laodiceans'. Epiphanius seems to know of some such letter by Paul, but regarded it as an extra letter, other than those already included in the Pauline Corpus; but the comments of Tertullian and his quotations from the epistle make it clear beyond doubt that what Marcion called 'Laodiceans' is the same letter which we know as 'Ephesians'.

We cannot here decide the unsettled question of the place of Philemon in the order of the letters as Marcion knew them. Epiphanius's placing of it, as being the more unusual, has a certain claim to be regarded as right, but we will treat it as coming last, without pretending to decide the issue either way. It makes little difference to the present argument, provided we may assume, with Knox, that if it were joined to Colossians, the title used to described them combined the names of two churches. We will also proceed on the assumption that in Marcion's list 1 and 2 Corinthians counted as one. unit, and also 1 and 2 Thessalonians, and that in these particulars Marcion is simply following the arrangement which he found in the original corpus.

If therefore we follow the order in which Marcion lists the epistles, and give the length of each one (reckoned by its number of pages in *WH*) we get this result: Galatians $8\frac{1}{4}$, Corinthians $40\frac{1}{2}$, Romans 26, Thessalonians $8\frac{1}{2}$, Ephesians $8\frac{3}{4}$, Colossians 6, Philippians 6, Philemon $1\frac{1}{4}$.

Harnack was satisfied that Marcion retained the order of the letters as he found it, with the exception that he took Galatians out of its original position in the middle, and put it first, because of all Paul's letters it was most congenial to the interpretation of the Christian message which he wished to spread. Harnack thought that in the original order Galatians followed Ephesians. In that case the order could be explained as a simple arrangement according to length, beginning with the longest. The one stumbling-block to this explanation is that Thessalonians precedes Ephesians instead of following it. Harnack thought that this anomaly could be removed by assuming that 1 and 2 Thessalonians, though treated as a unit, were nevertheless included as separate letters, and the inclusion of a title for the second letter would make the space occupied by the two letters rather more than that occupied by Ephesians. We have, however, already noted reasons for believing that the two Thessalonian letters were not separated, and that the opening greetings were omitted from 2 Thessalonians. If so, we may be sure that a second title would not be included. So Harnack's explanation of the one irregularity in what he took to be the original order is not wholly convincing.

Perhaps Harnack made a mistake in thinking that it was Thessalonians which was out of order. It might equally well be Ephesians which has been misplaced. This at any rate is the explanation which J. Knox accepts. He writes: 'A more likely explanation is that, when Marcion put Galatians in first place, it displaced Ephesians which had originally stood at the head of the corpus. Galatians is shorter than Thessalonians, but Ephesians is longer. Marcion's transposition of the two letters disturbed an originally "correct" arrangement' (*MNT*, p. 61).

If this suggestion is correct, it would mean that the original order of the collected letters was: Ephesians $8\frac{3}{4}$, Corinthians

E

40½, Romans 26, Thessalonians 8½, Galatians 8¼, Colossians 6, Philippians 6, Philemon 1¼. This would give Ephesians the status of an introductory letter, with the rest following, arranged in order of length. This appears to be a highly speculative hypothesis, and can only be entertained if further support is forthcoming.

A measure of support can be produced. No single item in it is very weighty, but cumulatively the items assume a certain impressiveness, even if they do not lead us beyond a somewhat guarded assent to the possibility of the truth of the hypothesis. Eight items will be noted, each adding its own small contribution to the weight of the whole argument:

(1) Almost certainly the first collection of Paul's letters would be issued in roll form. We saw reason to believe that Christians used the codex in publication at an unexpectedly early date, but we cannot assume this to have been before A.D. 100. We must proceed, therefore, on the assumption that rolls were used at least during the first century. So far as we know, the maximum size of the roll in general use was one which could contain such works as Matthew or Luke or Acts. Luke-Acts might well have been written as one single unit, had not the restriction of space, enforced by the roll's limitations, compelled the author to issue it in two parts. In pages from *WH*, Matthew requires 68, Luke 72, and Acts 71. Mark has 42 and John 53. It may be that Mark and John represent the more popular size of roll, and that the longer works are nearing the largest possible limit.[3]

Paul's letters comprise 99¼ pages, and we have no precedent to lead us to think that so much would be included in one roll. If, however, there had to be two rolls, one would expect them to be of approximately equal length. If Harnack's suggested order for the original collection is followed, it is difficult to know where the second roll would begin. If the first roll comprised Corinthians and Romans, that would amount to 66½ pages in *WH*, and leave only 32¾ for the second. If

---

[3] On the length of rolls, B. H. Streeter's judgement was: 'Both Matthew and Luke would have needed rolls of fully thirty feet long; and about twenty-five feet seems to have been regarded as the convenient length' (*FG*, p. 169).

Corinthians stood by itself in the first roll, the second roll would then contain the equivalent of $58\frac{3}{4}$ pages as compared with $40\frac{1}{2}$ in the first.

If Knox's suggested order is accepted, and Ephesians allowed to stand first, Ephesians and Corinthians would make up the first roll (with $49\frac{1}{4}$ pages in *WH*), and the rest the second roll (with 50 pages). That at any rate would make a very appropriate division of the whole into two approximately equal parts.

(2) The general character of Ephesians, which has led many critics to believe that it must have been a circular letter, and the omission of the name of any church in its opening greeting (in the earliest form of the text) is entirely in keeping with the position suggested for it by Knox and Goodspeed. As an introduction to the rest of the letters, its character is most satisfactorily accounted for. Every student of the epistle has recognized that among the Pauline letters it stands in a class by itself. The attempt to explain this peculiarity on the grounds that it is an encyclical letter is less satisfactory than the suggestion that it formed an introduction to the other letters (see Mitton, *EE*, pp. 250-1).

(3) One of the problems connected with Ephesians has been the change of name it assumes in Marcion's writings. To him it was 'The Epistle to the Laodiceans'. Those who interpret Ephesians as a circular letter, a copy of which was sent to many different churches, argue that a blank space would be left in the letter where the appropriate name of the individual church could be inserted; and that therefore different surviving copies of the letter would be addressed to different communities; and that Marcion knew the one addressed to Laodicea, whereas it was the copy for Ephesus which won its way into the accepted corpus. This would have been a satisfactory explanation had there been any evidence that copies with different names were known, or even if there had been any evidence that a blank space for a name was found in any of the manuscripts. But this is not so. In the earliest manuscripts there is no name, nor any blank space for a name. So the theory that suggests a number of variously inscribed copies is not satisfactory.

J. Knox therefore suggests the following explanation for the unusual name which Marcion adopted for this letter (*MNT*, pp. 61-2): Marcion found Ephesians standing first in the Pauline Corpus, but without any title or address, since it served as a general introduction to the seven letters that followed. He, however, wished to bring to the front of the collection the letter which he could use most convincingly to support his own novel contention, and the way he chose to accomplish this was to make a simple exchange, Galatians being brought to the front and Ephesians being put into its place, following Thessalonians. If the name 'Ephesians' had already been attached to this introductory letter, there is no reason why he should have wished to introduce another to replace it. But if it bore no name, because it was addressed to all Christians who would read the collected letters, a name would have to be found for it when it was removed from its original position. A letter associated with Laodicea is mentioned in Colossians 4[16], and that alone may have suggested the name to Marcion. Or the name of Laodicea may already have been connected with the combined letters of Colossians-Philemon, with which 'Ephesians' was closely linked. Both Epiphanius and the spurious Latin version of a letter of Paul to the Laodiceans bear witness to some tradition of a letter to that address, and this tradition may have influenced Marcion.

Tertullian, however, knows the epistle as '*Ephesians*', though his words suggest that in his copies the name of the church appeared only in the title and not in the text (*Adv. Marc.*, v. 17). He charges Marcion with making an arbitrary change of name in order to appear clever and original. But it is much more likely that Marcion was unaware of any claim that the letter was addressed to Ephesus. If, however, the corpus was first published at Ephesus, it is not surprising if the letter which stood first in the collection and bore no specific name should come to be associated with the name of Ephesus.

(4) We saw that Goodspeed is confident that Revelation shows clear indications of acquaintance with the Pauline Corpus. It echoes several, if not all, of the ten letters, and also by its epistolary introduction betrays the influence of the Pauline Corpus upon its writer. What else could have

induced him to take this novel step of introducing an apocalypse with seven separate letters addressed to seven individual churches by name, and one covering letter addressed to all the churches collectively? Nor is it only the idea of a collection of letters which fired his imagination. Even the number of letters in the revered collection seems to have affected him. He addresses seven letters to seven churches. So did Paul. Even if Philemon be reckoned as making one unit with Colossians, as Knox suggests, it is probable that the combination bore the twofold address 'To the Colossians and Laodiceans', so that the names of seven different churches would still be involved. Since, then, there is this probability that the author of Revelation not only took from the Pauline Corpus the idea of a collection of letters, but also the number of letters to be included, it is also quite likely that his use of a general letter of introduction, preceding the other seven, is based on the same model.

It must not be thought that the notion of some form of connexion between Paul's letters and the Letters to the Seven Churches is a mere fancy of modern critical ingenuity. The author of the Muratorian Canon took the similarity for granted, and even assumed that some kind of interdependence was the explanation of it. The language of the Canon is notoriously difficult to interpret accurately, but J. Knox says that the words relevant to our purpose 'tell us that "the Apostle Paul, following the example of his predecessor John", wrote to seven churches' (*MNT*, p. 54).[4] This Canon attributes the imitation to Paul. We, however, must attribute it to the author of Revelation, since the apocalypse is a later work than the letters of Paul. But at any rate it is clear that from early times the similarity was recognized and regarded as deliberate.

There is some evidence that to the people of ancient times the number seven represented completeness, and for that reason had a peculiar attraction for them. The representation

[4] The Latin Text of the Muratorian Canon at this point is recorded by Westcott as follows: '. . . *cum ipse beatus apostolus paulus sequens prodecessoris sui johannis ordine non nisi nomenati semptae eccleses scribat ordine tali . . .*' (*History of the Canon of the New Testament*, p. 534).

of the process of Creation as requiring seven days, and the established custom of the seven-day week are illustrative of this reverence for the number seven. A collection of letters to the number of seven would therefore in all probability have a certain special attraction of its own, as compared with six or eight.[5] It is possible that this attraction of the number seven was influential in the decision to combine the individual letters addressed to any one church into a single unit of correspondence. When, however, at a later date the three Pastoral Epistles were added, for ecclesiastical purposes, and thus the number seven was exceeded, there was no longer the same reason for retaining these large amalgamated units, and some of them were again divided up, where the original subdivisions could be easily detected, as between 1 and 2 Corinthians, and 1 and 2 Thessalonians. In other less obvious cases the combination of letters persisted, as within 2 Corinthians, and probably in Philippians.

(5) Another parallel to the Pauline Corpus is seen in the collected letters of Ignatius. Here again there are seven letters addressed to individual churches, and, in the form in which they were commonly circulated, one general introductory letter by Polycarp. The general plan followed in this compilation seems to have been provided by the Pauline Corpus. The presence of the introductory letter here, as well as in Revelation, may point to the presence of some such letter in the model which is being copied.

It is also worthy of note that in the most usual order of the Ignatian letters, the one to Ephesus stands first. This may have some significance, but it certainly cannot be pressed in view of the variation in the order of the letters in different manuscripts, and the uncertainty of the original order.

(6) Goodspeed calculates that Ignatius reveals acquaintance with all ten Pauline letters, except 2 Corinthians and 2 Thessalonians. The Oxford Committee is sure about his use of

---

[5] Streeter refers to this reverence for the number seven. Commenting on Clement's assertion that Paul suffered imprisonment seven times, that is three times more than Acts records, he writes: 'But Clement's arithmetic must not be pressed; "seven" is a sacred number into conformity with which Jews and Christians were always trying to squeeze facts' (FG, p. 532).

1 Corinthians, and almost sure about Ephesians, but uncon-vinced about the rest, though they acknowledge some evidence of similarities. P. N. Harrison agrees that 1 Corinthians and Ephesians are the only two Pauline letters about which it can be said with confidence that they were known to Ignatius. His knowledge of any others is to be regarded as doubtful (*PTE*, p. 235). What can, however, be said without fear of contradiction is that 1 Corinthians and Ephesians are the two epistles of which Ignatius had the clearest knowledge. If he knew others, and probably he did, he certainly knew them less intimately than he knew these two.

Various explanations have been suggested to account for this. Some think that 1 Corinthians had an individual circula-tion before its inclusion in the corpus, and so had been in Ignatius's possession for some time before the others, even before he left Antioch. Ephesians, too, may, for that matter, have come to his knowledge before he visited Asia Minor. Or, as Harrison surmises: 'The Ephesian collection of Pauline Epistles may have reached Antioch not long before the arrest of Ignatius. In that case he would have been able to look through them, and to retain in his memory the few odd phrases which appear in his letters; but he would not have had time to study them with the same thoroughness with which he had certainly studied 1 Corinthians. On this hypothesis the Epistle which we know as Ephesians would naturally have appealed to him with special force, as giving perfect expression to some ideas very near to his heart, particularly the ideas of Christian unity' (*PTE*, p. 246).

A variant explanation, with something to commend it, which harmonizes with what is here being suggested about the original order of the epistles, is that, if 1 Corinthians and Ephesians together made up the first roll, it may well have been that it was this roll which Ignatius had been able to read and study, either before leaving Antioch, or perhaps after his arrival in Asia Minor. The second roll came to his knowledge later, and received less careful attention, or else failed to win his interest in the same way that the two letters of the first roll had won it.

At any rate, it is not overstating the case to say that the

rather curious early preference for 1 Corinthians and Ephesians, not only on the part of Ignatius, but of other early
writers too, would be in accord with the suggestion that these
two epistles formed the first roll of the two-volume corpus, and
for that reason tended to receive more attention.

(7) The First Epistle to the Corinthians is a letter addressed
explicitly to the Christians at Corinth to help them to deal
with some of their own peculiar problems. It was written
partly in answer to a series of questions which had been sent to
Paul, and partly as a result of certain disquieting reports about
the church there, which had come to Paul's ears. The opening
words of the address are quite appropriate to such a situation:
'To the Church of God which is at Corinth, even them that are
sanctified in Christ Jesus, called to be saints.' But what is
surprising in so intensely individual a letter is the additional
sentence which follows: 'with all that call upon the name of
our Lord Jesus Christ in every place, their Lord and ours'
(1 Co 1[2]). It is difficult to believe that these further words
stood in Paul's original letter. With the contents of 1 Corinthians before us, it is well-nigh impossible to believe that Paul,
as he wrote it, visualized its going to all the churches everywhere, or that he would wish so particular, and in some ways
almost private, a letter, to be given universal circulation.

Several scholars have felt that the added words must have
been introduced when the corpus was formed and 1 Corinthians was given first place in its order. They argue that the
change was made because then 1 Corinthians 1[1] was the
opening sentence not only of its own letter, but of the whole
corpus, and therefore required modification so as to make it
include all Christian readers. This might be interpreted as
evidence against the suggestion that Ephesians stood at the
head of the corpus. But it would be equally appropriate for
some such modification to be introduced into the opening
sentences of the first letter which followed the special introduction. Even if Ephesians stood first, purposely written for that
position, the editor might well have felt the wisdom of inserting
also into the opening sentence of the first individual letter a
few words which would indicate the universal interest and
applicability of all that followed.

These added words therefore may rightly be taken as evidence that among the letters to the individual churches 1 Corinthians was placed first, but that does not preclude the further suggestion that Ephesians preceded them all, as a general introduction addressed to all readers everywhere, and free from all local limitations.

(8) J. Knox has given careful study to the Muratorian Canon, and in particular to the order in which the Pauline letters are listed there (*MNT*, pp. 53ff). It is a most baffling order, and one might be inclined to conclude that it has no explanation except the jumbled memory of the scribe, although the fact that he deliberately names the letters as first, second, third, etc., almost suggests that he is copying from a list. The order of the letters in this Canon is: Corinthians, Ephesians, Philippians, Colossians, Galatians, Thessalonians, Romans. In addition we are told that Paul wrote to Philemon and Titus and twice to Timothy, and that there are two letters to Corinth and two also to Thessalonica.

The date of the Muratorian Canon is probably at least fifty years later than Marcion. It would not in itself, therefore, occasion surprise to find that Ephesians had been displaced from the head of the list by Corinthians. It is a much shorter letter, and once it had come to be thought of as a letter to one church, and had lost its character as a general introductory epistle to the whole collection, it would have forfeited its right to priority. Nor is it surprising to find Philemon separated from the church letters and grouped with the Pastorals, which are also addressed to individual persons. 'But,' writes Knox, 'what rhyme or reason can be found in the order of the other letters: Philippians, Colossians, Galatians, Thessalonians, Romans? . . . Perhaps it is the result of an early attempt to place the letters in their chronological order' (*MNT*, p. 71). This last suggestion seems most unlikely, and Knox does not advocate it as a probable explanation. He then proceeds to call the reader's attention to a 'very curious fact'. He disclaims it as a probable solution, but it is so ingenious that it almost deserves to be the correct solution. He suggests that it may just be possible that the scribe derived his list of the Pauline letters from a copy of the corpus in two rolls, but for some reason approached each roll from its last page instead of its first. Perhaps the rolls had been read through and not unwound again. So taking up the first roll, and starting from the end, he enters first Corinthians and then Ephesians. Then turning to the second roll, and working again from the end, he enters first Philippians and last Romans. Curiously enough, if this were the right explanation, it would mean that these two rolls contained the Pauline epistles in the order which Knox, on other grounds, believes to have been original. He adds: 'This supposition is probably altogether too fanciful, but that one of our two earliest lists of the letters of Paul—that of Marcion—indicates an order in the original collection which our other earliest list exactly reverses is, to say the least, interesting.'

The theory, then, that Ephesians was written as a kind of Introductory Letter to the first published collection of Paul's letters is entirely consistent with the character and contents of Ephesians. The epistle reads like a deliberate attempt to summarize Pauline doctrine, which in the genuine letters is spasmodic and unco-ordinated. In it the doctrine is lifted above episodes of merely local or antiquarian interest, and is given a setting of universal application. The uncertainty in the early Church of the precise church to which it had been addressed, and the omission from our earliest manuscripts of the name of any church at all, may also be quoted as supporting this theory. Perhaps even its prominence in the writings of the Apostolic Fathers (surpassing, apparently, even that of Romans) points also in the same direction.

Whether it can be successfully argued that it actually stood first in the first published Corpus, as an Introductory letter presumably would have done, is much less certain. There are, it is true, some curious scraps of evidence that it might quite possibly have done so, but they are very far from being conclusive.

It is the kind of writing that might have been meant for an Introductory Letter, but whether it ever actually was one, and held the position proper to such a letter, is more than can be claimed with any degree of confidence.

CHAPTER EIGHT

CONCLUSIONS

W E HAVE considered various questions which arise in connexion with the Pauline Corpus, and the circumstances of its first formation. We have asked: How did it first come into being? and When and where was it made? We have inquired what were its precise contents at the time of its first appearance, and in what order the individual letters were arranged. We have speculated whether it may even be possible to surmise who first envisaged the feasibility of collecting the letters together, and undertook the enterprise, and carried it to a successful completion in actual publication.

None of these questions can be answered with complete assurance, and to some of them it seems almost presumptuous to attempt any answer at all, so slight is the reliable evidence. We do not, for instance, know who first collected the letters. All we can say is that some guesses about his identity are less unlikely than others. We cannot confidently determine the original order in which the letters were arranged, or whether Ephesians did actually stand first among them (as we should expect, if it was produced specifically to serve as an Introduction). Such evidence as is offered in support of that claim is exceedingly fragmentary and wholly circumstantial.

It may well be, however, that the publication of the Acts of the Apostles was in some way the occasion which prompted the formation of this Corpus. It is also more than probable that in its earliest form it did not include the Pastoral Epistles.

Three other conclusions, however, can be named, which have a far greater measure of probability about them, even if they too do not achieve the level of complete certainty. They are:

(1) The letters of Paul did not creep gradually into the life and worship of the Church, but sprang suddenly into the

consciousness of the Christian community, about a generation
after they had first been written, and in such a way as to
suggest that they had been deliberately collected and then
published as a Corpus, after a considerable period of almost
complete neglect.

(2) This first collection took place about A.D. 90.

(3) It was carried into effect in or near Ephesus.

APPENDIX

Ignatius ad Eph. ii.

Concerning Burrhus, my fellow bondservant, your minister* under God, everywhere well-spoken of, it is my request** that he remain† beside me, to the credit†† both of you†† and of the Bishop.

Philemon 13

. . . whom I would** have retained† with me, that in thy stead†† he might have ministered* unto me in the bonds of the gospel.

Ignatius ad Eph. iii.

I do not enjoin* you, as if I were someone.** For though I have been a prisoner*** for His name, I have not yet been made perfect. . . . But since love† does not allow me to be silent about you, for this† reason I preferred to beseech†† you.

Philemon 8-9

Wherefore, though I might be much bold in Christ to enjoin* thee that which is convenient, yet for love's sake† I rather beseech†† thee, being such a one as Paul the aged**, and now also a prisoner*** of Jesus Christ.

GENERAL INDEX

INDEX OF SCRIPTURE REFERENCES